SPEAK TO YOUR HEART

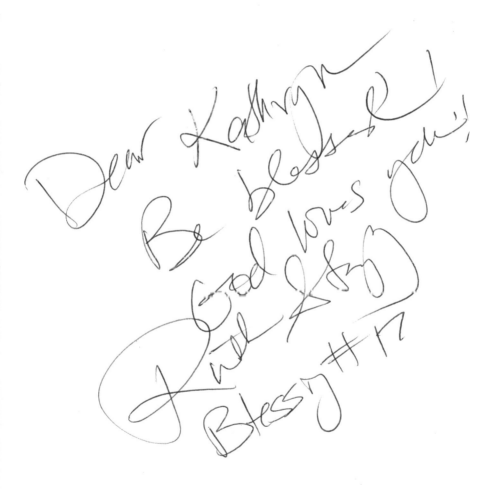

Speak to Your Heart

70 Biblical Blessings to Encourage and Challenge Yourself and Others

Ruth Stingley

Full Circle Press

Printed in the USA.

For other information: www.speaktoyourheart.com

Published by Full Circle Press
Orange, CA 92869

ISBN 978-0-615-98691-3

Typesetting services by BOOKOW.COM

Songwriter and artist Michael W. Smith read a blessing he wrote over his audience at the conclusion of one of his concerts on an Alaskan cruise. The results were unexpected to him. Smith writes about the experience in his book titled *A Simple Blessing: The Extraordinary Power of an Ordinary Prayer* (Zondervan, 2011). He had so many requests for the blessing that he began reading it over all his audiences.

Smith spoke biblical truth in a format that personally encouraged others. What we speak is a manifestation of what is in our hearts. Luke 6:45 illustrates this: "A good man out of the good treasure of his heart brings forth good; and an evil man out of the evil treasure of his heart brings forth evil. For out of the abundance of the heart his mouth speaks." And James proclaims that "out of the same mouth proceed blessing and cursing. My brethren, these things ought not to be so" (James 3:10). The impact of our words has obvious spiritual significance.

Scripture also urges us to "consider one another in order to stir up love and good works, not forsaking the assembling of ourselves together, as is the manner of some, but exhorting one another, and so much the more as you see the Day approaching" (Hebrews 10:24-5).

This book is unique in that one of its purposes is to be read aloud to others. Sylvia Gunter and Arthur Burks' *Blessing Your Spirit* (Birmingham, AL: The Father's Business: 2005) provided inspirational fodder for the layout of this book. Their read-aloud blessings are unique and personal.

Speak to Your Heart can best be described as a composite of verbal devotionals (and exhortations), and its purpose is for encouragement of self and others, which is why blanks are provided throughout each "blessing" for the inclusion of a name (yours or another's). Read them for encouragement. Speak these short, Scripture blessings over yourself or a loved one. Pray them. Live them.

*For ideas on how to use or to read how these blessings impacted people, some testimonies are given in italics after specific blessings. Additional thanks to Debbie Miller, Karin Metoyer, Brittany Futrell, Susan Wachtel, Bev Spurlock, Rachel Golino, Barbara Burlew, Susan Parker, Deb Rydman, Frankie Galaway, Nikki Andrews, Debbie Stingley, Robyn Bolton, D'Ann Conner, Sarah Mittmann, Janelle Simons, Sandy MacGinnis and others for providing these.

Acknowledgements

To my husband, Jeff—a most wonderful blessing from God who worked with me throughout the process of writing this book and researched the theology behind these biblical blessings/ encouragements (and who wrote the last one). You make my heart sing!

To my children—all blessings from God—Joshua, Rachel, Elizabeth and Abbey. You are my inspiration and have challenged me to live and speak out these blessings.

To my parents, Allen and Vicki—who encouraged me to write and never stop encouraging and loving me.

To my dear in-loves, Norm and Merilynne—who have gifted me with their love and their son.

To my siblings: Ellen and Jon, Vikki and Greg, John and Andie, Diane and Juan, Debbie and Mark—I couldn't ask for better; how blessed am I!

To my incredible Monday ladies and special friends who have walked with me through this writing process and have listened and prodded me to keep on keeping on! You inspired me to write many of these. Forever grateful to you all.

To my Jesus—who trumps all, has ransomed me with His own blood and who owns me. I can't ever repay, but I will bless Your name forever and ever! I pray that these blessings will encourage others to rise up and bless You!

CONTENTS

INTRODUCTION

"Why are you cast down, O my soul? And why are you disquieted within me? Hope in God, for I shall yet praise Him for the help of His countenance." Psalm 42:5

In this verse in Psalm 42, David is having a conversation with his soul and telling himself not to be downcast. Before that, it's not the most pleasant-sounding conversation, as David is dealing with the harsh reality of what is happening in his life. But it turns when David chooses to rely not on his own outlook and devices, but instead questions his demeanor and tells himself it's about time to get in touch with God's promises and His Word.

The following excerpt from D. Martyn Lloyd-Jones' book, *Spiritual Depression: Its Causes and Cure*, highlights the vital necessity of speaking to ourselves and ends definitively with Psalm 42:5. Lloyd-Jones writes: "Have you realized that most of your unhappiness in life is due to the fact that you are listening to yourself instead of talking to yourself?

"Take those thoughts that come to you the moment you wake up in the morning. You have not originated them, but they start talking to you, they bring back the problems of yesterday, etc. Somebody is talking. Who is talking to you? Your self is talking to you" (Spiritual Depression, 20).

Lloyd-Jones continues by emphasizing David's talk to himself in Psalm 42:5. He writes: "Instead of allowing this self to talk to him, he starts talking to himself. 'Why art thou cast down, O my soul?' he asks. His soul had been depressing him, crushing him...You have to take yourself in hand, you have to address yourself, preach to yourself, question yourself...And then you must go on to remind yourself of God, Who God is, and what God is and what God has done, and what God has pledged Himself to do.

"Then having done that, end on this great note: defy yourself, and defy other people, and defy the devil and the whole world, and say with this man: 'I shall yet praise Him for the help of His countenance, who is also the health of my countenance and my God' " (*Spiritual Depression*, 21).

Speak to Your Heart provides seventy biblical blessings that you can use to speak to your own heart or from your heart to others. Proverbs 4:23 issues a warning: *"Keep your heart with all diligence, for out of it spring the issues of life."* Solomon's wisdom to value and protect your mind, emotions and will is, in fact, what you seek to do as you speak and pray these blessings over yourself. Speak them over others, and you will impart God's wisdom to their hearts.

Each blessing is Scripture-infused and devotional in nature. Some were written for specific situations; others are more general in nature. What you will find is that the topics that concern most believers are covered: fear, hope, insecurity, worry, love, prayer, etc. While by no means exhaustive, these blessings will have meaning to yourself and to individuals in your life.

I wrote these blessings over a two-year span. I was, obviously, well acquainted with them and had read them to and over several people. So, when I underwent a particularly challenging time, I thought that perhaps they would be less meaningful to me. *Not so.* God often highlighted specific ones for me to read and pray through—and I was ministered to and encouraged afresh.

Be intentional and personal with the blessings. The word "bless" used in these entries has a multitude of meanings. Consider it interchangeable with "encourage," "exhort," "urge" or "pray." Whether you speak these "blessings" to yourself or someone else, the end result is for the benefactor to be blessed with spiritual growth, maturity, wisdom and encouragement.

My prayer is that the words in these blessings—read silently to yourself or spoken aloud with compassion and an intent to bless others—will touch each and every recipient.

BLESSING 1: DANCE OF DELIGHT

_____, listen with "ears that hear" the Word of God for you: *"Delight yourself in the Lord, and He will give you the desires of your heart"* (Psalm 37:4). God is delighted when you choose to delight yourself in Him. It's a bond built on trust as written in the preceding verse: *"Trust in the Lord and do good; settle in the land and feed on faithfulness."*

I encourage you, _____, to go deeper in your trust level with the Lord, so deep that your heart will begin to dance with delight as you think upon God's faithfulness and react with joy in your daily duties.

I bless you, _____, with lightness in your step as you choose to dance through the same old chores, because your heart is listening to the voice of the Father, whispering, "I'm with you even in these"—and you smile with satisfaction. Even if your first steps of the joy dance are faltering, your Abba Father takes pleasure in your attempts.

I bless you, _____, with the melody and lyrics of *"Great is Thy faithfulness, O God my Father. There is no shadow of turning with Thee. Thou changest not; Thy compassions they fail not"*—resonating deep in your soul and spirit as you face challenges that rock your world.

And I bless you, _____, with holding out your hands to the One who redeemed you—body, soul and spirit—and choosing to let Him lead you in a sweet dance of surrender that will keep you on your toes in anticipation, for He who called you is faithful and will satisfy your every heart's desire as you delight in Him.

I bless you in the name of Yeshua, Jesus of Nazareth, Who poured out His life blood so that you could dance with Him in delight throughout all of eternity.

Notes (anything I need to do/think differently/consider who needs to hear this, etc.):

Testimonial/feedback: "These blessings have blessed my heart and met me right where I'm at in the moment I needed them. They are truly a gift. I love writing in my journal the date I read them and going back and seeing how the Lord has spoken to me through each one. So powerful! And I don't keep them just to myself; sharing with those who are on my heart has also been a blessing.

Blessing 2: Life Perspective

Life can be looked at in a variety of ways; however, as a Christian, we either choose to view life from the *"dead man"* or the *"new man"* perspective. _____, according to Galatians 2:20, *"I have been crucified with Christ; it is no longer I who live, but Christ lives in me; and the life which I now live in the flesh, I live by faith in the Son of God, who loved me and gave Himself for me."*

I bless you, _____, with living from a new-man perspective, where your first response to anything in this world is an otherworldly, Christ perspective.

When trials come, you'll see joy in the journey and counteract the pain with *"Christ in you, the hope of glory."* When people misunderstand you or talk about you behind your back, you will choose to pray for them and bless them. When the days seem like drudgery and the future dim, your faith will rise as you counteract complaining by choosing to rejoice, pray and give thanks.

_____, you are called to live life to the fullest. In worldly terms, that means getting the most out of life to satisfy you and bring circumstantial happiness. In new-man terminology, it means being so full of the Spirit that joy and peace and hope overflow from your life into the lives around you.

I bless you, _____, with not settling for anything less than the fullest measure of the Spirit. I bless you with forward movement and upward vision so that your steps are in line with God's kingdom agenda. And I bless you to show your true colors that can only come from rejoicing often in your new birth and tackling life with ABUNDANT LIFE.

I bless you in the name of Yeshua, Jesus of Nazareth, who gave His life to bring you up from the grave to LIFE EVERLASTING.

Notes (anything I need to do/think differently/consider who needs to hear this, etc.):

BLESSING 3: NO LONGER ORPHANS

"I will not leave you orphans; I will come to you," Jesus promised in John 14:18. _____, Jesus foretold of the indwelling Holy Spirit. I bless you with a growing desire to allow the Holy Spirit to reveal Himself to you as the Helper God intended. As a New Testament believer, you have the incredible blessing of God not just with you but WITHIN you.

So I bless you with an "inside-out" life, whereby the inner work of the Spirit is on display in a marvelous way for all to see.

_____, to become one who is full of the rivers of Living Water, you must continually empty yourself, decreasing so Christ may increase. I bless you with such a strong identity as God's beloved child that any opportunity given to you to empty yourself so you can be filled will be seen as a joyous occasion.

Take heart, _____, for you are called to live a life of abandon, free from the worldly pulls of self-indulgence and self-satisfaction—with a single-eyed focus on the Lover of your soul.

I bless you, _____, with being so in tune with the Holy Spirit that you whistle as you walk, calling others in to experience the fullness of life that you have been granted. I bless you to proclaim freedom to those still trapped in orphanages, holding your adoption papers close enough for them to see the signature of your Father written in the blood-red beauty of Christ's sacrifice.

And I bless you, _____, to spill out all the Spirit's fruit as you live a life of inside-out, fully blessed and fully emptied, then fully filled again in anticipation of being used over and over as an ambassador of Christ.

I bless you in the name of the Father, who adopted you; in the name of Jesus, who promised not to leave you as an orphan; and in the name of the Spirit, who indwells you forever in power.

Notes (anything I need to do/think differently/consider who needs to hear this, etc.):

BLESSING 4: PEACE PERSONIFIED

"Peace I leave with you; My peace I give to you," proclaimed Jesus in John 14:27. *"Not as the world gives do I give to you. Do not let your heart be troubled, nor let it be fearful."* _____, Jesus offers peace that is not sullied by earthly definitions.

The world hands out a temporary reprieve from circumstantial distress and labels it "peace." It feels good for a moment, but such peace never lasts and never sets your heart at rest. The peace Jesus spoke about is not temporary reassurance, but heart insurance. For God says that His peace will guard your heart and mind in Christ Jesus (Philippians 4:7).

I bless you, _____, with discerning the difference between the two with ease. I bless you with enjoying a temporary reprieve from stress that can be labeled "peaceful" but only banking on God's peace to overcome an unsettled heart.

_____, I bless you with choosing to come to God with all your problems before you ever consider bringing them up to anyone else.

I bless you with bathing your requests in thanksgiving to God who promises that He not only listens to the cries of His children but He also answers.

And I bless you with such a deep trust in the One who covenants with you for life that your heart and mind remain insulated from fear.

I bless you, _____, with a heart that sings in tandem with the God of peace and speaks His language of peace that penetrates and puts to end all anxiety, fear and failure.

I bless you in the name of the Father; in the name of the Prince of Peace—His Son; and in the name of the Holy Spirit, who exudes the fruit of peace as you surrender to God's will, God's way.

Notes (anything I need to do/think differently/consider who needs to hear this, etc.):

Testimonial/feedback: "What I especially appreciate about the blessings is that they help bring my focus back on God, not looking at my circumstances or inability to handle what I'm going through on my own. The blessings are directly from Scripture and have helped me to see how huge God is and to know His character as He has revealed Himself in the Bible. The blessings remind me that nothing is too hard for my heavenly Father, and He is for me and not against me. I'm reminded about who I am in Christ, what He's done and continues to do for me and the Holy Spirit who indwells me. I find the blessings help lift my eyes and set them upon the LORD."

BLESSING 5: CALLED TO BLESS

"Bless the Lord, O my soul," begins Psalm 103, *"and all that is within me, bless his holy name! Bless the Lord, O my soul, and forget not all his benefits, who forgives all your iniquity, who heals all your diseases"* (Psalm 103:1-3, ESV).

I bless you, _____, with the impetus and inclination to bless the Lord at all times.

In these three short verses, we are called to *"bless the Lord"* three times. When Scripture repeats something twice, it's for a definitive purpose. When it repeats three times, as in Revelation 4:8 when the four living creatures around the throne cry out, *"Holy, holy, holy,"* we are to stand up and take notice.

So I bless you, _____, with standing up in your spirit and blessing the Lord with all that is within you! I bless you to stand in awe of the One who bleeds forgiveness from His very core and who never stops forgiving when we repent, even past seventy times seven.

I urge you to be a generous blesser, not a reluctant or halfhearted or even complacent one.

And I bless you, _____, to recall easily all the varied and beautiful benefits God pours into your life—past, present and future—and to inscribe them in great detail on your mind and heart.

When the enemy pulls one of his "Let's-question-God" cards, I bless you to trump him over and over with God's benefit cards you have in hand.

You never lose when you keep God's goodness to you at the forefront of your mind and heart, and I bless you to be quick to respond to every situation with living examples of God's blessings that will obliterate the enemy's lies.

I also bless you, _____, to not place limits on God's intent to heal all your diseases.

The word "diseases" encompasses more than physical affliction and incorrect functioning of our bodily systems and organs. I bless you to experience God's heart to heal you completely—mind, body, soul and spirit. His forgiveness heals your spirit and paves the way to bring wholeness to every part of you.

As Psalm 103 continues, the psalmist David recounts that God redeems your life from destruction, crowns you with lovingkindness and tender mercies and satisfies your mouth with good things so that your youth is renewed like the eagle's (verses 4-5).

I bless you to live out all these promises of God as if they were spoken afresh every morning with great fervor and inspirational anticipation. LIVE them in the power of the Spirit!

So, in light of the incredible blessings God has bestowed on you and has promised to you, _____, I bless you to forever bless the name of the LORD God Almighty, who forgives, heals, redeems and energizes and to whom belongs all glory, honor, power and blessing now and forevermore.

Notes (anything I need to do/think differently/consider who needs to hear this, etc.):

BLESSING 6: RECEIVE THE CHILDREN

_____, Jesus said in Luke 9:48: *"Whoever receives this little child in My name receives Me; and whoever receives Me receives Him who sent Me. For he who is least among you all will be great."*

I bless you, _____, with the call on your life to see little ones with the Father's eyes and seek to protect those who are dear to the Father's heart. I bless you with childlike vision that results in gaping astonishment at what Abba Daddy can and does do for you and through you.

And I bless you to walk in humble dependence as your Father takes your hand and leads you *as* He knows and *where* He knows best on an adventure that He has orchestrated for you.

When Jesus made this statement about receiving a little child in His name, it was in response to His disciples disputing who would be greatest in the kingdom of heaven. Jesus chose to respond with a real-life example by calling a child into their midst before answering.

At that time, a child in Jewish culture was not afforded much attention, let alone considered "great," so Jesus silenced their rumblings with God's "upside-down" kingdom view.

So I bless you, _____, with such like-minded perception of Christ's purposes that God seldom has to redirect your mind to line up with His. I bless you to join in God's championing of children at the same time that He schools you in "upside-down" theology that continually takes God at His Word over man's.

And I bless you to traverse the narrow path, trek to heights of steep-cliff proportions with hinds-feet help, deflect aimed arrows with the pitted buttress of a faith shield held stalwartly in place, and dance with all the God-wonder that set into motion David's acclaim as a man after God's own heart.

I bless you, _____, in the name of GOD ALMIGHTY —Maker of heaven and earth—and the One True God who holds your heart so that it gleams with an intensity and purity worthy to reflect His majesty.

Notes (anything I need to do/think differently/consider who needs to hear this, etc.):

BLESSING 7: TAKE HEART

_____, listen carefully to the following words Jesus spoke in John 16:33: *"In the world you will have tribulation; but be of good cheer, I have overcome the world."* Although Jesus spoke this encouragement to His disciples, it is inscribed in Scripture for us as well.

_____, in this short sentence is the crux of life. I bless you with pulling from Jesus, the Word of Life, what you need on an hourly basis, on a daily basis and for your lifetime—on time, never early and never late. I bless you with encouragement that always looms larger and more brilliant than any dark night or dark thought.

And I bless you with an ever-increasing realization of this verse so that you are never taken unawares by what is unfolding in your life.

You will have tribulation. It's not a possibility but a given. Affliction and suffering will come your way. You will not escape them, for the world's offerings stand in stark juxtaposition to what God offers.

In the words directly preceding, Jesus says: *"These things I have spoken to you, that in Me you may have peace."* Jesus speaks so that peace is the result; the world speaks, and distress is the outcome. I bless you, _____, to rise above every suffering and affliction with the peace of Jesus that pervades and puts tribulation in its place. I bless you with this promise of peace that preempts every blow the enemy plans and prevents anxiety, worry and fear from holding you captive.

"Be of good cheer" is your turning point, _____, that takes tribulation and sets it in its proper place. It cannot overcome your spirit. It cannot paralyze your heart. Unless you let it by forgetting the promise that is yours.

I bless you, _____, to emblazon Christ's words on your heart and mind. I bless you to take them to heart and choose to rearrange your circumstances instead of agreeing with your circumstances. I bless you to take your stand next to the One who has given His lifeblood for you and whose promises are always valid with no expiration date.

And I bless you, _____, to look full in the wonderful face of Jesus so that every trial dims in the brilliant LIGHT of His countenance. I bless you in the name of Yeshua, Who offers nothing less than the BEST for you and proved it with His last breath upon the cross, for He alone is completely trustworthy. Take heart, _____, for He has overcome the world.

Notes (anything I need to do/think differently/consider who needs to hear this, etc.):

BLESSING 8: SHELTERED SECURELY

"He who dwells in the secret place of the Most High shall abide under the shadow of the Almighty. I will say of the Lord, 'He is my refuge and my fortress; my God, in Him I will trust.'" (Psalm 91:1-2).

_____, I bless you to be sheltered in the name of the Lord God Almighty—who is your refuge and your fortress—because your trust level in Him rises high above all fear. Fear sometimes comes calling when you least expect it. It bears upon your mind and infiltrates your heart.

But God has promised to insulate the hearts of those who seek to dwell under His covering, in His secret place where the foe is banished.

So, I bless you, _____, with a passion to stay long and stay secure in the presence of the Lord who desires for you to tarry with Him. I bless you to hearken your hearing to listen to the decibels of the One on whom you depend. I bless you to hear Him call you *beloved* in the familiar tones of a Father with whom you have conversed often and not just in frenzied interchanges of desperate need.

I encourage you to ask questions that have nothing to do with your circumstances and everything to do with who God is—so that your questions are eclipsed in the majesty and glory of GOD Himself.

And I bless you to be as satisfied with a response of sweet silence as you are with an invigorating exchange of exhortation and encouragement.

When you live in such communion with God, you cannot help but speak aloud of Him, so I bless you to say often that *"He is my refuge and my fortress; my God, in Him I will trust"* (Ps. 91:2).

I bless you never to remain silent when presented with an opportunity to vocally proclaim God's glory and goodness. And I bless you with never-ending occasions to speak out of the overflow of your present communion with God so that others see and hear that God IS—not was or will be—ALL in ALL to you and that your trust level is settled now and forever.

_____, I bless you in the name of the ONE TRUE GOD, who forever is and will be your refuge, your dwelling place and your strong tower.

Notes (anything I need to do/think differently/consider who needs to hear this, etc.):

Testimonial/feedback: "I have been the recipient of many of the blessings written by Ruth. When they have been read over me, I feel as if Jesus and Ruth love and cherish me— and that He is drawing me closer to Him."

BLESSING 9: PRECIOUS INDEED

Inscribed in Scripture are the following words that have consoled and encouraged many a soul: *"Precious in the sight of the Lord,"* writes the psalmist in psalm 116, verse 15, *"is the death of His saints."* _____, for God so loved you that He gave His only begotten Son to die for you. You are of incredible value.

God Almighty knows your frame, saw you when you were sequestered in the womb of your mother months before you were born, can count each hair on your head on any given day, knows the intimate thoughts of your heart and can speak the words you intend to vocalize before they roll off your tongue. Moreover, He has kept you from danger more times than you can count, for He has given His angels charge over you to keep you in all your ways (Psalm 91:11).

_____, you were born into the time and place the Lord designated for His distinct purposes. He has blessed you with life. He put a song into your heart with distinctive notes that only you could sing to achieve the melody that would bring to life what God desired. He wove your giftings and longings into a vibrant quilt of joy that inspired and comforted many, and His design of you is a beauty to behold. _____, you are precious to the Lord.

I bless you, _____, to see with spiritual eyes the glory set before you. I bless your heart to overflow with thanksgiving for the many gifts you've been given and to understand—if even in the smallest way—that your life and testimony are His (God's) story in the making, and their impact will reach beyond your generation for a ripple effect of spiritual proportion.

_____, precious (important and of no light matter) in the sight of the Lord is the death of His saints. When the moment comes for God to call you home, _____, you will begin to fully understand the meaning of precious.

I bless you with a heart fully entranced and fully ready to meet the One who redeemed you, who called you out of darkness into light. And I bless you with a glorious anticipation that floods your heart and mind with the presence of the Prince of Peace Himself so that your ears strain to hear the welcome call of the One who sacrificed all for you to enjoy abundant life FOREVER.

I bless you in the name of the Father, who created you; in the name of Jesus, His Son, whose blood brought you into the family; and in the name of the Spirit, who indwells you and is eagerly awaiting your introduction to GLORY!

Notes (anything I need to do/think differently/consider who needs to hear this, etc.):

Testimonial/feedback: "I'll never forget the time exactly when we were saying goodbye to my grandma—how the Lord used you to speak to me through prayer and blessings."

BLESSING 10: THE HAND OF THE POTTER

_____, I bless you to draw strength from the following words written by Isaiah in chapter 64, verse 8: *"But now, O LORD, You are our Father; we are the clay, and You our potter; and all we are the work of Your hand."* Your life is being molded by One whose qualifications are exemplary.

Yet there would be little comfort if the One in charge of your destiny was only noted for His ability to craft remarkable endings. Isaiah preempts that concern by calling Him Father; and, I bless you, _____, with the unshakeable peace that comes from knowing that God, your *Father,* is in charge of you and your life story.

I bless you, _____, with being pliable in the hands of the Potter so that He can begin the process of molding the masterpiece He has in mind. I bless you to be fixed on Jesus, so that you are properly centered for the Potter to fully attend to His creative venture. And I bless you to not just endure, but to enjoy the slow and steady hand of the Father as He carefully crafts you so that you will not be torn apart.

_____, for you to become all that He foresees will take time. I bless you with keeping your heart in concert with the Father's timing, focused on His vision and His intent for you.

The Potter knows exactly what He intends for you to become, and He knows the perfect amount of pressure needed. Furthermore, His eye has to be on you the entire time for the desired outcome.

So I bless you, _____, with knowing that the vessel you are becoming is for the Father's own use and is therefore precious to Him. I bless you with the excitement that comes from understanding that your life is vital to the Father's kingdom plans. I bless you with seeing the compression as God's hand of approval, and I bless you with freedom to live wholeheartedly in sync with the Potter whose eye and hand is on you for good at all times.

I bless you, _____, in the name of the Father—the Potter—who is transforming you from glory to glory to be a shining replica of His Son on display for the world to see.

Notes (anything I need to do/think differently/consider who needs to hear this, etc.):

Testimonial/feedback: "The truth of the blessings speaks to me profoundly and helps me to switch my perspective to God's kingdom perspective."

BLESSING 11: GOD'S GOOD FOR YOU

_____, as you listen to this passage that you most likely have heard, read, and quoted often, I bless you to hear it anew with ears tuned to the Father's meaning.

_____, "...*we know that all things work together for good to those who love God, to those who are the called according to His purpose*" (Romans 8:28). This verse is sandwiched between the Apostle Paul's discourse on the sufferings of this present time and his recounting of God's great love for us culminating in his declarative statement that NOTHING can separate us from God's love.

I bless you to comprehend God's heart in every circumstance you are undergoing, and I bless you, _____, to continually respond to any trial with a strong declaration of God's love.

Many quote Romans 8:28 without giving time or credence to the conditions listed, proclaiming that ALL things work together for good...period. Even though they quote the whole verse, their emphasis remains on the first part.

According to the truth presented in Romans 8:28, all things DO work together for good to (1). those who are His; and (2). to those who love Him. As His child, one condition is already fulfilled through Jesus. I bless you, _____, to always have the other condition fulfilled by your heart overflowing with love for God.

When trials come, I bless you with a first-response declaration of: "I love You, God!" I bless you to draw nearer and more intentionally to Jesus when your days and nights shine with brightness and glory. Then, when circumstances bring difficulty or sorrow, your heart will be overcome with love for the One who promises to work it out for good for you.

I bless you with such a strong foundation of love that any shaking will only reinforce your resolve that God is for you and that good WILL be the result. Oh, _____, speak Romans 8:28 with such confidence in your spirit that even the enemy won't try to question your rock-solid love for Jesus that is based on the love God has for you in calling you His own.

I bless you in the name of the Father, who called you; the Son who brought you into the family through His blood sacrificed on the cross; and the Spirit, who inspired Paul to end this chapter with the following words of life: *"For I am persuaded that neither death nor life, nor angels nor principalities nor powers, nor things present nor things to come, nor height nor depth, nor any other created thing, shall be able to separate us from the love of God which is in Christ Jesus our Lord"* (Romans 8:38-9).

Notes (anything I need to do/think differently/consider who needs to hear this, etc.):

BLESSING 12: REJOICE AND...!

_____, *"rejoice always, pray without ceasing, in everything give thanks; for this is the will of God in Christ Jesus for you"* (1 Thessalonians 5:16-18). Isn't it encouraging that the search for God's will for each of us leads to this medley of triumph?

I bless you, _____, to never venture anywhere unless you are committed to remaining in rejoicing, praying and thanksgiving. I bless you to plumb the sweet depths of discovering new joy in Jesus. I bless you to stay settled in constant interaction with God, and I bless you with thanksgiving permeating not just some of your days and ways, but EVERY one.

While the details of your life will change, staying true to this admonition in 1 Thessalonians 5 will transform those details into an ever-expanding panoply of Christ's glory evident in your heart to spill over into others' lives.

I bless you, _____, to draw from the never-ending supply of the Spirit so that your words and your countenance shout CONTAGIOUS JOY to the world. That will happen only when you walk continually in cooperation with the Lord, freely offering up your questions, hopes, dreams, hurts and life in a rich exchange, listening more readily than speaking, loving more easily than striving.

I bless you to limit human interaction when it propels you away from joy and thanksgiving and instead choose to dwell in the presence of the Lord. I bless you with an abiding life of peace in Jesus that saturates your soul in increasing measure.

And, _____, I bless every cell of your being to respond in thankfulness, to live from an overflow of grace that percolates joy into your own life and that of others. Living in joy positions you in the spotlight of God's favor, and thanks will be the song you belt out with praise projecting from your heart and lips at all times. For this is God's will for you! His will for you is joy, communion and grace.

I bless you, _____, in the name of the Father, Son and Spirit, whose three-in-one presence emboldens you to rejoice always, pray without ceasing and in everything give thanks.

Notes (anything I need to do/think differently/consider who needs to hear this, etc.):

Testimonial/feedback: "Every blessing that you have shared with me has spoken to me. It is a personal message that reminds me that I am loved, or that there is something I need to work on, or think about. The Scripture verses send me back to my Bible to learn more and hear more of what God has to say to me."

BLESSING 13: NO FEAR!

When God makes a point in His Word to clearly spell out His replacement for a negative, we are blessed if we commit it to memory and to action. In 2 Timothy 1:7, the Apostle Paul states, *"For God has not given us a spirit of fear, but of power and of love and of a sound mind."*

I bless you, _____, with identifying and calling out fear in your life. It often masquerades as worry, anxiety, concern, sleeplessness, compulsive habits—or a multitude of other negatives—in order to stay beneath the surface of your understanding. I bless you with intentionally bringing it into the light so God's truth can destroy its power.

Fear is addressed multiple times in Scripture, and it has gripped many—biblical heroes included. Because fear as a negative is given so much attention in the bible, it's likely that no one has escaped its hold at some point in their lives.

But God calls out with clarity: "I did not give you a spirit of fear. It's not from Me." Fear is from the enemy and surrenders power to him by allowing him access to one's mind and leaves one feeling loveless.

So I bless you, _____, to confess with a contrite heart any disposition toward fear. I bless you to lay each and every hold on it that the Spirit brings to mind before God. He forgives readily and offers a remarkable replacement. And God's substitution for the enemy's hold is incredibly astonishing.

Therefore, _____, I bless you to fully comprehend the wonder of God's "instead-of" giftings. The enemy offers fear; God INSTEAD blesses with power, love and a sound mind.

I bless you to walk in God's power that pulverizes fear. I bless you to bask in His lavish love that strips fear of its propensity to live a life of "less than." And I bless you to dissemble every "lie trap" that the enemy slyly sets and plunder his power with the sound mind God has gifted you.

I bless you, _____, to so obliterate fear with these three gifts that you become a formidable force against the enemy and a mighty warrior used by God to liberate those held captive by fear. I bless you in the name of God Almighty, who has made a provision for every obstacle that you face through Jesus who triumphs over the foe victoriously!

Notes (anything I need to do/think differently/consider who needs to hear this, etc.):

Blessing 14: Majority Rules

_____, listen to the Word of God written in Psalm 18: 34-5: *"For who is God, except the Lord? And who is a rock, except our God? It is God who arms me with strength, and makes my way perfect."* And now listen to the words penned by David in Psalm 68:35: *"O God, You are more awesome than Your holy places. The God of Israel is He who gives strength and power to His people."*

What a comfort that we have God on our side. What a joy that God is with us and in us! I bless you, _____, to fervently proclaim with the Apostle Paul in Romans 8:31: *"If God is for us, who can be against us?"*

Paul is not laying a premise for unlimited favor with people in this passage; instead, he is declaring the unlimited love of God with which we can stand in complete assurance.

I bless you, _____, to rise up to the fullness of God's heart for you in all things. I bless you to peer above the bar of earthly limitations and gaze upon God's greatness and majesty. I bless you to look not at the step in front of you but at the One who leads you out of complacency and into an adventure where He is the Author and Director and you follow His script.

With God, you are *always* in the majority. _____, I bless you to speak out of the overflow of intimacy with God, and along with the psalmist David shout aloud for all to hear: *"The Lord my God will enlighten my darkness. For by You I can run against a troop, by my God I can leap over a wall. As for God, His way is perfect; the word of the Lord is proven; He is a shield to all who trust in Him"* (Psalm 18:28b-30).

And I bless you, _____, to step out of the crowd of loneliness, insecurity and insufficiency and exult in God, whose promises never tarnish and whose presence transforms you into a God-focused, God-confident, God-blessed and God-loved majority of one plus ONE! I bless you in the name of God Omnipotent who reigns forever and ever, world without end.

Notes (anything I need to do/think differently/consider who needs to hear this, etc.):

Testimonial/feedback: "As I read and re-read your blessing, I humbly received encouragement and reminder of the strength and shield that God is. I have been looking at just getting by one step at a time; in some ways that is good, yet I love hearing, 'I bless you to look not at the step in front of you but at the One who leads you out of complacency and into an adventure where He is the Author and Director and you follow His script.'

"Thank you for always speaking truth over me and blessing me. As I look back over this past year, I marvel at the consistent pursuit of the Lord's love in speaking relentless truth over the lies and deep injuries of the past."

BLESSING 15: A DOUBLE DOSE +

_____, listen to the prayer the Apostle Paul prayed in Ephesians 3: 14-19: *"For this reason I bow my knees before the Father, from whom every family in heaven and on earth is named, that according to the riches of his glory he may grant you to be strengthened with power through his Spirit in your inner being, so that Christ may dwell in your hearts through faith—that you, being rooted and grounded in love, may have strength to comprehend with all the saints what is the breadth and length and height and depth, and to know the love of Christ that surpasses knowledge, that you may be filled with all the fullness of God"* (ESV).

I bless you, _____, to let this prayer penetrate deep in your heart until it begins to cry out for fulfillment. I bless you to see circumstances in view of the dimensions of God's love, allowing the extraordinary extension of His heart to overwhelm what threatens to overwhelm you.

And I bless you to find markers of God's love throughout your day. List them in extensive detail on your heart until they are indelibly inscribed and you can revisit them often and hold them up in their brilliance against any darkness that would come your way.

Real understanding of the immensity of God's love for you has to precede being filled with all the fullness of God. Fullness of God. Let that phrase settle deep in your heart.

I bless you, _____, to never be satisfied with a single dose of knowing God's love that may only lead to an eighth of a filling. I bless you to seize the full portion with the measure of faith God has granted you and rejoice in the abiding presence of Christ in you, the hope of glory.

I bless you to long for and petition for and thank God for His immeasurable love that never runs dry, never comes up empty and that is your blessing here, now and for all eternity.

I bless you, _____, in the name of the One *"who is able to do far more abundantly than all that we ask or think, according to the power at work within us, to him be glory in the church and in Christ Jesus throughout all generations, forever and ever. Amen"* (Ephesians 3:20-21, ESV).

Notes (anything I need to do/think differently/consider who needs to hear this, etc.):

Testimonial/feedback: "This is one of the blessings I received that has impacted my life. In it, I was challenged to find 'markers of God's love throughout your day.' I took this to mean that I should find something to remind me of His great love for me—so that when I see it—my mind immediately is drawn to how much I am loved by my heavenly Father. I chose a bird singing. So when I hear a songbird, I direct my heart to remembering His love for me. It has been about a year now that I have been doing this.

"The past year has been a difficult one for our family with many struggles. Having this constant reminder in my day has helped me to never lose sight of the fact that even when things are not going well, God's mercy and lovingkindness for me is constant and unending. Of course, I don't always tune in to hear the birds; but, when I do, my heart is immediately redirected to praise to the Father for His wonderful loving care of me."

Blessing 16: Mind-Dwelling

_____, God's advice is superb and always rewarding when put into practice. And when it revolves around what we think, we have plenty of opportunities to practice, for our minds are rarely silent.

Therefore, I bless you, _____, to overhaul your thought life in accordance with God's Word in Philippians 4:8 regarding this topic: *"Finally, brethren, whatever is true, whatever is honorable, whatever is right, whatever is pure, whatever is lovely, whatever is of good repute, if there is any excellence and if anything worthy of praise, dwell on these things"* (NASB).

It's quite easy to gloss over this passage as a simple addendum to the Apostle Paul's admonition in the prior verses to exchange our anxieties with prayer and thanksgiving. That exchange is linked to God allowing His peace to guard our hearts and minds in Christ Jesus.

And this passage is also inextricably linked to those verses. We allow God to be the sole key-holder in guarding our hearts when we follow His wisdom on what is to fill our minds.

So I bless you, _____, to allow God free reign in your thoughts as you choose to dwell on what is right and noble and just. I bless you with a purity of mind and heart that makes a conscious choice to disregard and decimate all base thoughts and enemy-inspired lies.

I bless you to curtail any compromising mind-meanderings. Instead allow Scripture to so saturate your world that it surfaces in your talk and your walk.

_____, I bless you to so over-think on God and His majesty, His supremacy, His overarching love, His rich abundance of mercy, His grace-displaying favor and His glory-filled presence that all other thoughts dim in the splendor of Christ—and you are overcome with thoughts that turn mourning into joy, despair into praise and ambivalence into ardor for Jesus.

I bless you in the name of Yeshua, who ransomed you from a life of destruction and put a new song into your heart, your mind and your mouth!

Notes (anything I need to do/think differently/consider who needs to hear this, etc.):

Testimonial/feedback: "When Ruth first started writing blessings, she gave me one for my husband. I took it home and read it to him. He said it 'really hit home.' He was so touched that he asked for the copy and put it in his Bible. Every so often I would see him take it out, read it again and smile."

BLESSING 17: MORE THAN BIDING TIME

_____, Jesus said the following to His disciples, and it is inscribed in His Word for us also: *"I am the true vine, and My Father is the vinedresser. Every branch in Me that does not bear fruit, He takes away; and every branch that bears fruit, He prunes it so that it may bear more fruit. You are already clean because of the word which I have spoken to you. Abide in Me, and I in you. As the branch cannot bear fruit of itself unless it abides in the vine, so neither can you unless you abide in Me"* (John 15:1-4, NASB).

You are a fruitful branch, _____, and so you have been through times of pruning that are painful but necessary. I bless you to look at those times and note God's deep handprint on each one.

I bless you to trace over the furrows of the indentation He left behind and realize that the valleys were places of greater dependence upon Him.

Pruning involves removal for a healthy, more abundant outcome. In natural terms, it goes against human nature to prune beautiful fruit-producing branches, but an astute gardener chooses to forego the lesser for the superior harvest.

So I bless you, _____, to rejoice that pruning is not a sign of disapproval but of God's validation. I bless you to memorize each pruning lesson—and purpose to add your notes of praise to the Pruner for His careful extrication of the lesser for the greater result.

Abiding is your pruning protection, _____, and the guarantee of a fruitful yield. As Jesus says in John 14, you will be pruned —instead of removed—if you are fruitful, and you can only bear fruit if you abide in Him. So your pruning means that you are abiding, and *abiding* in biblical terms is a continual loyalty that takes a stalwart stand even in the face of disappointment and betrayal.

Therefore, I bless you, _____, to embrace abiding in Christ as a lifelong pursuit of mammoth proportions. I bless you to cling with desperate longing and eager anticipation.

I bless you to not consider any season of your life to be just *"biding time"* but instead to extricate the spiritual value inherent in every day that you have life and breath so that Christ is as glorified in the hours you find difficult as in the moments that are intensely satisfying.

I bless you to lean heavily on Jesus not only when you feel the world is against you but also when you walk in full-fledged favor with man.

And I bless you, _____, to sit, walk, skip, run, sing and dance through your days and nights in the fullness of a lifelong heart commitment to abide without reserve and with the fullness of extravagant joy.

I bless you in the name of Jesus who called you from darkness to life to live an abiding life that far surpasses what you could ever envision because HE has triumphed over sin, death and the enemy and is your Redeemer for all time!

Notes (anything I need to do/think differently/consider who needs to hear this, etc.):

Testimonial/feedback: "I sent this blessing to a couple who spends hours praying diligently for people. The husband responded that it was exactly what he needed, and that he had just preached a sermon on the very same topic. He said that he would be re-reading it many times to encourage his heart."

Blessing 18: A Hearing Heart

_____, listen with ears intent on hearing the Lord's words in Mark 4:24-25: *"And he said to them, 'Pay attention to what you hear: with the measure you use, it will be measured to you, and still more will be added to you. For to the one who has, more will be given, and from the one who has not, even what he has will be taken away'"* (ESV).

This admonition is enclosed between numerous parables Jesus spoke to the crowds, and it follows this verse: *"If anyone has ears to hear, let him hear"* (v. 23). Jesus speaks out this statement eight times in the gospels, declaring that if you have "ears to hear," then hear!

I bless you, _____, with hearing that is tuned to the cadence and beauty of God's voice. I bless you to receive His word of gladness and make a deliberate choice to mull it over in your mind until you can speak it forth with clarity and conviction. And I bless you with spiritual perception to make a heart connection with the words of the Lord so they will traverse readily from your mind to heart and back again with ease.

Jesus also cautions: *"Take heed what you hear."* _____, I bless you to be vigilant with what you allow in your ears, mind and heart. I bless you to "tune out" worldly wisdom, enemy lies masquerading as truth-in-part, self-talk that demeans and advice that detours you from God's heart and intent. I bless you to instead soak in and savor the simplicity and wonder of the gospel.

I bless you to grasp the glorious grandeur of God and pore through His Word with unparalleled passion to discover more. I bless you to see His creative hand in the world and enjoy His expressions of inspiration given to others.

God's promise is that more will be given to those who hear, and I bless you, _____, with the Word of life becoming so alive in your day-to-day encounters that you wake up excited about the God adventures in store for you. I bless you with drawing from the wellspring of the Word-made-flesh again and again and proving that God's Word never returns void and never comes up empty but instead explodes with vitality and meaning.

I bless you to be a living illustration of whatever God has put on your heart to study in His Word so that others will "read" your walk and draw close to hear what God has done for you.

And I bless you, _____, to so entwine your ears with God's heart that your hearing will be sensitive to the still, small voice of the Spirit and that you will treasure beyond measure your "hearing time."

I bless you, _____, in the name of Jesus of Nazareth, the Word who came in the flesh to bring hearing to the spiritually deaf so we can hear with clarity His every whisper, salutation, sermon and song.

Notes (anything I need to do/think differently/consider who needs to hear this, etc.):

BLESSING 19: TIME REDEMPTION— WISE REFLECTION

_____, listen to the Word of God written under inspiration of the Holy Spirit to the Apostle Paul in his letter to the church at Ephesus: *"Therefore be careful how you walk, not as unwise men but as wise, making the most of your time, because the days are evil. So then do not be foolish, but understand what the will of the Lord is"* (Ephesians 5:15-17, NASB).

Earlier in the same chapter, Paul encourages the believers to live up to their calling as *"children of light."* _____, I bless you with eyes that peer through the cloudiness of the world with the radiant vision you have been granted as a child of light. I bless you to glean from the Spirit the necessary wisdom for your next day, your next challenge, your next encounter with darkness.

I bless you to walk forward with purpose, not with flippancy or frustration—but to instead press on as God's presence within catapults you past choices that would hold you captive.

The words *"making the most of your time"*—also translated—*"redeeming the time"* hold a treasure trove of meaning for believers, as God is the Master at redeeming time. He has woven redemption throughout time and eternity with the blood of Jesus poured out on your behalf in His triumph over death and the devil.

So I bless you, _____, to not only celebrate the redemption of your life and spirit, but to also rejoice in the redemptive subplots that God has written into your life story. I bless you to see your mistakes rewritten as character developments in later chapters. I bless you to trace your trials through to the triumphant ending God intends.

I bless you to watch the foreshadowing of failures being transformed into faith builders, and I bless you, _____, to continually search and find the Savior's touches of grace and mercy for you and for those whose lives are woven into your narrative.

Finally, _____, I bless you to make every moment memorable in light of Jesus' example of redemption. I bless you to walk out the gospel in your own heart and life. I bless your will to be so in step with God's will that the enemy flees as light clashes with darkness, forgiveness fends off anger, kindness covers over malice and love trumps wrath.

I bless you in the name of Jesus, the Redeemer of all time, forever to be praised for His redemptive work in your life and mine!

Notes (anything I need to do/think differently/consider who needs to hear this, etc.):

Testimonial/feedback: "I had read a few of the blessings to my son, and he was touched on several occasions, so I wasn't completely surprised when he asked for copies of nineteen of the blessings and inserted the names of the girls in the sister dorm wing at the Christian college he attended. I helped him roll them up and put a ribbon around them, and he handed them out on Valentine's Day. He was amazed at how many of the girls came up to him and told him how meaningful they were to them. He was thrilled and felt blessed himself."

BLESSING 20: DELIVERANCE AND DELIGHT

_____, the psalmist David speaks often of God's deliverance. Psalm 18 is one such tribute to God's power in personal peril. Listen to the words David penned in verses 18 and 19 of that psalm: *"They confronted me in the day of my calamity, but the Lord was my support. He also brought me out into a broad place; He delivered me because He delighted in me."*

I bless you, _____, to see God's hand of deliverance in both prevailing providential acts that build your faith and in quiet calming circumstances that restore your countenance. I bless you to face any confrontation with the rock-solid reminder that the Lord is your support, and His help will never let you down or leave you defenseless.

David adds an *"also"* to his song of deliverance when he says that the *"Lord brought him out into a broad place."* A broad place in biblical times refers to being out in the open, away from the taunts and the terror of the enemy.

So I bless you, _____, with deliverance that leads you into the brilliance of light where the enemy has no place to hide. I bless you with celebrating the wide expanse of God's mercy in coming to your aid. And I bless you with marveling at God's expertise in how He leads you from confinement to liberation.

In verse 19, David remarks that the reason for his deliverance was due to *"delight."* As God delighted in David, I bless you with the same confidence that David had in attributing God's movement on his behalf to being favored by God. It's one thing to experience favor from people and something on an entirely different plane when God delights to show His love for you.

I bless you to witness the interlocking dynamic of God's deliverance and delight often. I bless you to recount each deliverance experience with jubilation, to boldly speak of God's power and presence to deliver.

And I bless you to encourage others to join in your joyful refrain of glory to God. I bless you, _____, in the name of God Almighty, whose powerful hand rescues you from darkness and transports you to a broad, bright and beautiful place of freedom.

Notes (anything I need to do/think differently/consider who needs to hear this, etc.):

BLESSING 21: TRIO OF LIFE

_____, the book of Colossians begins with a great reminder of our life in Christ. Listen to the words recorded by the Apostle Paul in Colossians 1:3-6: *"We give thanks to God, the Father of our Lord Jesus Christ, praying always for you, since we heard of your faith in Christ Jesus and the love which you have for all the saints; because of the hope laid up for you in heaven, of which you previously heard in the word of truth, the gospel which has come to you, just as in all the world also it is constantly bearing fruit and increasing, even as it has been doing in you also since the day you heard of it and understood the grace of God in truth"* (NASB).

Paul distinctly refers to hope, faith and love—and commends the believers in Colossae for their love for the saints connected with their faith in Jesus because of the hope laid up for them.

I bless you, _____, with faith, hope and love being the primary characteristics that define your life. I bless you with a strong faith in Jesus that proclaims to those watching that He is your Redeemer, your King, and the One whom your soul loves. I bless you to cling to Jesus in times of trouble and triumph.

And I bless your trust level in Jesus to increase exponentially as you maneuver through life with a radiant countenance that beholds the One who has ransomed you from depravity and darkness.

Faith in Jesus demands action, and the Apostle Paul links such faith to a love for all the saints. I bless you, _____, with the complementary action of love that faith begets. I bless you to breathe and bestow love for all the saints, with no partiality and no pretense. I bless you with an overflow of the heart of God so that your actions reflect a thought life that is aligned with a God focus.

I bless you to color outside the lines when it comes to creatively revealing God's love to others and that your active pursuit of loving the saints will stand out to the world.

Finally, _____, I bless you to agree with the Apostle Paul that the hope of heaven is indeed the beauty of the gospel and the stimulus for a life that bears fruit. I bless you to live with that hope stirring your heart, deepening your faith and escalating your love for all the saints. And I pray that you experience the rewarding pleasure of other believers who are thankful for your faith, hope and love—and who covenant to lift you in prayer.

I bless you in the name of the Father, in the name of the Son and in the name of the Spirit—who prod you onward to the upward calling of a life of faith, hope and love.

Notes (anything I need to do/think differently/consider who needs to hear this, etc.):

BLESSING 22: THE BLESSING OF BEING FORGIVEN

_____, listen to the words David inscribed in Scripture after he had been confronted with his sin by Nathan, the prophet: *"Create in me a clean heart, O God, and renew a steadfast spirit within me. Do not cast me away from Your presence, and do not take Your Holy Spirit from me"* (Psalm 51:10-11).

This *"man after God's own heart"* was concerned with more than forgiveness; what he petitions God for illuminates why he was aligned with God's heart.

I bless you, _____, to be so captured in heart, mind, soul and spirit by God's heart that your legacy will be one of great spiritual proportions. I bless you to be likened to David in his propensity to get right with God. I bless you to never wallow in sin but to eliminate it from your life and make ample room for the Holy Spirit to thrive.

David knew that if he allowed his sin to fester in his heart, he would estrange himself from the only One who could bring healing and restore wholeness. Forgiveness encompasses more than mere mental assent to God's choice to not hold sin against us because of Jesus' ultimate sacrifice on our behalf.

So I bless you, _____, to have the joy of salvation restored every time you confess your shortcomings before God. I bless you to not allow confession to sink you deep into depression but instead to restore rejoicing in and through your very being.

I bless you to be so upheld by the Holy Spirit that the culmination of confession is pure joy.

No sin is outside God's willingness to readily forgive. So I bless you, _____, with all the wonder that can permeate your heart and soul as you revel in the understanding that God, who knows your every thought and action, forgives you when you confess.

And God's forgiveness, _____, has the creative power to restore purity and passion to a broken and contrite heart. So I bless you with a profound sense of His purpose for and His tenderness toward you as you enter His presence with humility and a hunger for His touch of compassion.

I bless you, _____, with experiencing His creativity in re-making your mistakes into illuminations of His glory. And I bless you with a response of gladness and delight that speaks so highly of a God of sweet reconciliation that others will be irresistibly drawn to Him and that you will forgive as readily as you have been for-given.

_____, I bless you in the name of God, the Deliverer and Healer, who came to regenerate broken hearts and broken lives in the cleansing blood of Jesus so that He would become your life song sung at full volume for all to hear!

Notes (anything I need to do/think differently/consider who needs to hear this, etc.):

Testimonial/feedback: "I have reflected upon Psalm 51 in the past, so when this blessing was read to me, it brought me back to a focus on the

Bible. I think I usually see forgiveness in earthly terms, knowing how hard it is for me to forgive at times and often experiencing conditional forgiveness from others. So this blessing restored hope for me and others and enabled me to see God's desire for a heart broken over sin but open to being restored."

BLESSING 23: FORGOTTEN? NOT!

_____, you have most likely heard the following words in Scripture so often that the meaning has lost its impact. I bless you to enjoy a renewed sense of their value for your life as you listen with awakened ears.

Jesus says in Luke 12: 6-7: *"Are not five sparrows sold for two pennies? And not one of them is forgotten before God. Why, even the hairs of your head are all numbered. Fear not; you are of more value than many sparrows"* (ESV).

I bless you, _____, to see yourself in light of God's love for His creation—for God's awareness encompasses the most menial of creatures, and His notice of us includes the most insignificant details. I bless you to live your days in the expanse and extravagance of God's attention of you and for you.

I bless you to uncover remarkable occurrences where God lavishes His affection on you by proving His incredible consideration of all that you are and all that concerns you. And I bless you to treasure each remembrance with rejoicing—and to reflect your worth upward in praise to the One who made you.

These two verses are quoted in two gospels: Luke and Matthew. And in those two gospels, they occur in the very same order as to what Jesus says directly before and directly after. Before the sparrow analogy, Jesus speaks about not being afraid of men but to instead only fear God. After, Jesus contrasts what happens to those who confess Him (Christ) before men to those who deny Him.

I bless you, _____, to relish the context in which God places your value. I bless you to relinquish your fear of man, to fully revere God and to respond with open profession of your praise to Him before all. I bless you to realize that value and fear cannot coexist.

Your Creator reveals His incredible love for you and admonishes you to banish fear, so I bless you to allow His orchestration of your life to harmonize the difficult with the delightful so that no overtones of fear can disrupt the melody He has gifted you to play.

I bless you to respond to God's incredible picture of your value to Him by magnifying His glory with great awe and reverence, and I bless you, _____, to *"confess"*—profess openly, to praise and celebrate—God for His magnificence, wonder, majesty, power, protection, glorious grace, redemptive mercy and luminous love.

I bless you to carry your worth as only a child of God can: with boldness, bravery and brilliance.

I bless you, _____, in the matchless name of the MOST HIGH GOD, who endows you with great value so that you have the courage to confess Him before men.

Notes (anything I need to do/think differently/consider who needs to hear this, etc.):

BLESSING 24: EYE ON YOU

_____, listen with expectancy to the words written in Matthew 6:26-30, as spoken by Jesus: "*Look at the birds of the air, that they do not sow, nor reap nor gather into barns, and yet your heavenly Father feeds them. Are you not worth much more than they? And who of you by being worried can add a single hour to his life? And why are you worried about clothing? Observe how the lilies of the field grow; they do not toil nor do they spin, yet I say to you that not even Solomon in all his glory clothed himself like one of these. But if God so clothes the grass of the field, which is alive today and tomorrow is thrown into the furnace, will He not much more clothe you? You of little faith!*" (NASB).

Jesus chooses two carefree objects—birds and lilies—to illustrate His tender care of His creation. I bless you, _____, to pull from this well-known passage what is pertinent to you and your personal life.

I bless you to not only shelf worry but to hold it up against the God-worth you've been granted and to give it no place in your heart, mind and thoughts. For God wants your heart to reflect His. So I bless your heart's capacity to enlarge and to embrace God's vision of you and for you.

In verse 30, Jesus introduces the need for greater faith to catapult you from worry to the worth God freely bestows on His loved ones.

I bless you, _____, to unceasingly weave God's value into your heart so that it serves as a supreme faith-builder that bursts into your circumstances with kingdom clarity. I bless you to herald the One who has clothed you with honor and life and considers you the apple of His eye, as He describes His children in Deuteronomy 32:10.

While Matthew 6 reiterates that God's eye is on the sparrow and the lilies for their good, He saves His tender descriptions of love for His children. His eye is not only on you, _____, but His eye is filled with affection and admiration, your Abba Father's continual look of love.

I bless you to not shy away from God's gracious and glorious focus. I bless you to bask in His singular affection that has elevated you to be seated with Christ in the heavenly places (Ephesians 2:6). And I bless you to gaze back at God with unequaled adoration and unrivaled adulation.

I bless you in the name of God Almighty, whose incomparable eye is on you without fail forever and a day.

Notes (anything I need to do/think differently/consider who needs to hear this, etc.):

Testimonial/feedback: "These blessings have been such a source of encouragement to me and others that I have seen ministered to by them. They remind us of our identity and bring life to our spirit. These are a practical way of applying Ephesians 4:29 and powerfully impart grace to the recipient. I recommend this as an important resource to anyone who desires to speak life and encouragement over others."

BLESSING 25: MAJESTY IN MIND

_____, I encourage you to listen and to reflect on the following words inscribed in Scripture in Luke 9:43: *"And they were all amazed at the majesty of God."* In reference, this statement speaks of the crowd's response to Jesus rebuking the demon in an epileptic boy and healing him. Jesus' disciples had been unable to help the boy, and the boy's father was distraught.

Only Jesus came to his rescue. And the crowd? They marveled and were amazed at the majesty on display in front of them.

I bless you, _____, with multiple experiences of Jesus responding in a majestic way to your needs. I bless you with not settling for human assistance when it's clear that your circumstances require a God-sized answer.

I bless you with a desperation born of dependence upon the Only One who can come to your aid, and I bless you with His rescue birthing a response of astonishment that revolutionizes your emotions, your thoughts, your heart and your actions.

Back to Luke 9: *"But while everyone marveled at all the things which Jesus did, He said to His disciples, 'Let these words sink down into your ears, for the Son of Man is about to be betrayed into the hands of men'"* (verses 43b-44).

Jesus took the adulation of man in stride, for He knew that the marvel of the crowd was transitory and would soon take a macabre turn toward murder. I bless you, _____, with a *"turn-around"* reaction to man's approval of you by rotating your attention toward our majestic God to gauge His countenance and receive His validation.

I bless you to seek His face, His righteousness and His kingdom. And I bless you to point with precision toward the One who gifted you and enables you to be a blessing to others.

I bless you, _____, to major on the majesty of God, and to release your heart to sing with abandoned praise with David in Psalm 145:5-6 when he proclaimed: *"I will meditate on the glorious splendor of Your majesty, and on Your wondrous works. Men shall speak of the might of Your awesome acts, and I will declare Your greatness."*

And I urge you to keep your mind fixed on the peerless and preeminent might of God who has endowed you with the superlative ability to glorify Him as supreme in your heart and life.

I bless you, _____, in the name of our Majestic God *"who is able to keep you from stumbling, and to present you faultless before the presence of His glory with exceeding joy. To God our Savior, Who alone is wise, be glory and majesty, dominion and power, both now and forever. Amen"* (Jude 24-5).

Notes (anything I need to do/think differently/consider who needs to hear this, etc.):

Testimonial/feedback: "What a great reminder to keep my focus on Jesus! I read this blessing several times until I 'got it' and purposefully turned my thoughts from my problem at hand to my God!"

BLESSING 26: ABUNDANT ASKING

_____, Ephesians 3:20-21 speaks of God's super-abundant response to our requests: *"Now to Him who is able to do exceedingly abundantly above all that we ask or think, according to the power that works in us, to Him be glory in the church by Christ Jesus to all generations, forever and ever. Amen."*

I bless you, _____, with the *"more mindset"* that God brings to light in these two verses. God always comes through with more, not necessarily more things—especially if things consume you—but more of what is essential for your wellbeing.

The Apostle Paul asked that those in Ephesus would be strengthened with might through God's Spirit, that Christ would dwell in their hearts through faith, and that they would be so rooted and grounded in love that they would be able to grasp the love of Christ and be filled with all the fullness of God.

And Paul was convinced that God would answer the prayer beyond anything their minds could conceive.

I bless you, _____, to ask for that very same outrageously incredible inner power so that you would be propelled toward faith-filled living. I bless you to ask in the same vein that Paul did, with confidence in the answer, so that the life and love of Christ would surge throughout your mind, body, soul and spirit.

Need strength? Your weakness and dependence will be the catalyst for His strength to carry you on wings of eagles.

Need peace? I bless you to lay your worries and fears at His feet so that He can crush them as He takes you in His arms and embraces you so intently and intimately that guarding your heart and mind in Christ Jesus is inescapable.

And I also bless you to not doubt the delivery of God's answers (as God's ways aren't on the same plane as our thinking and His timing is often not in beat with our measure of understanding).

Instead, I bless you to approve God's abundant answers as being rooted and grounded in love for you. And I bless you to rejoice as excitedly in the immediate double-delightful responses as well as any questionable turn-of-events that points you upward toward the over-abundant outcome.

I bless you, _____, in the name of GOD ALMIGHTY who waits for you to ask for more of Him and His love and His power so that He can respond with blessing upon blessing of in-credible proportions that will take your breath away and replace it with Life Himself.

Notes (anything I need to do/think differently/consider who needs to hear this, etc.):

BLESSING 27: WALK WORTHY

_____, listen with an open heart to the following words given by inspiration of the Holy Spirit to Peter in 1 Peter 1:6-7: *"In this you greatly rejoice, though now for a little while, if need be, you have been grieved by various trials, that the genuineness of your faith, being much more precious than gold that perishes, though it is tested by fire, may be found to praise, honor, and glory at the revelation of Jesus Christ."*

I bless you, _____, with the view and vision of Peter, who called forth believers to a walk of glory paved with stones of re-membrance, splinters of trials and road signs of rejoicing.

I bless you to walk the path of faith that those before you have traveled, with the victory destination held clearly in mind. And I bless you to move in step with Jesus as your portion of strength and resilience to advance with worship in your heart and praise on your lips.

Your faith will be tested, _____, and I bless you not to just withstand each trial but to discover the depth of your devotion to God who desires your faith to be proved genuine.

I bless you to uncover beauty in the midst of hardship. I bless you to find God's favor when circumstances appear adverse. And I bless you to advance spiritually despite physical delays because God is for you, completely for you—without reserve—and He alone determines your worth.

The Apostle Paul in Ephesians 4:1-3 calls all believers *"to walk worthy of the calling with which you were called, with all lowliness and gentleness, with longsuffering, bearing with one another in love, endeavoring to keep the unity of the Spirit in the bond of peace."*

This *"walk worthy"* admonition comes on the heels of Paul's prayer for believers to be rooted and grounded in the love of Jesus, to be filled with all the fullness of God and to realize God's abundant ability to go above and beyond all we ask or think.

I bless you, _____, to walk worthy, with head held high because God has gifted you with Himself in great love. I bless you to walk worthy from the inside out, blessing others with the outrageous love you have been granted. I bless you with the peace of God penetrating your heart and overflowing into the lives of those whom God is using to test your faith.

And I bless you with the patience that the Spirit endows so that your walk results in a glorious testimony of the One who walked the road to Calvary for you to follow Him.

I bless you in the name of Jesus of Nazareth, who for the joy set before Him, endured the cross, despising the shame, and *"whom having not seen you love. Though now you do not see Him, yet believing, you rejoice with joy inexpressible and full of glory, receiving the end of your faith—the salvation of your souls"* (1 Peter 1:8-9).

Notes (anything I need to do/think differently/consider who needs to hear this, etc.):

Blessing 28: Morning Song

Listen, _____, to the Word of God written by David in the first two verses of Psalm 108: *"O God, my heart is steadfast; I will sing and give praise, even with my glory. Awake, lute and harp! I will awaken the dawn."* These two verses have been called *"The Warrior's Morning Song,"* as David praises God and proclaims that his heart is strong before he enters the day's duties and conflicts.

I bless you to join David in choosing to fix your heart in confident expectation on God alone. Even if the day ahead may be dimmed by discouragement, I bless you with the sweet surrender of a heart that looks beyond the natural and stands under the shadow of the Almighty in whose presence no foe can stand.

I bless you, _____, to rise up in adoration, setting up your banner in Jehovah's name so that the name of the Lord looms larger than any other proclamation that could disrupt your day. I bless you with the garment of praise that provides protection against the spirit of despair.

After David begins with praise, he proceeds to petition God with believing prayer. Praise takes David into the courts of God, allowing him to step through with confidence in what God will do.

I bless you, _____, to arrange your days with praise and petition in that order. I bless you to sing of God's greatness with such loud acclaim that the heavens will open to sing in concert with your melody. I bless you to uncover so much more with which to laud God that your petitions diminish in size. And I bless you with praise that emanates from your spirit with such force that your faith escalates in like proportion.

David ends the psalm with a resolve that only comes from a steadfast heart: *"Give us help from trouble, for the help of man is useless. Through God we will do valiantly, for it is He who shall tread down our enemies"* (Psalm 108:12-13).

I bless you, _____, to conclude your prayers with the assurance David displayed. I bless your faith to match your praise so that the majesty of God overshadows all doubt, and fear succumbs to His perfect love for you. God is FOR you!

May the promise and certainty of God's valiant help resonate through every minute of your days and nights so that glorious praise radiates from you at all times.

I bless you, _____, in the name of Jehovah, who has stamped His name upon your heart so that you can begin every morning with the clarion call of praise that rings forth with faith in a God worth celebrating!

Notes (anything I need to do/think differently/consider who needs to hear this, etc.):

BLESSING 29: GOD'S PERSONAL BLESSING

_____, listen with ears ready to hear the word of the Lord written in Numbers 6:22-27: *"Then the Lord spoke to Moses, saying, 'Speak to Aaron and to his sons, saying, 'Thus you shall bless the sons of Israel. You shall say to them: The Lord bless you, and keep you; the Lord make His face shine on you, and be gracious to you.   The Lord lift up His countenance on you, and give you peace.' So they shall invoke My name on the sons of Israel, and I then will bless them'"* (NASB).

It doesn't get better than hearing the exact words of blessing that God desires to speak over His children, so I bless you to let each word penetrate your heart and speak volumes of meaning to your soul.

"The Lord bless you and keep you." As God's child, you are privy to His blessing and His keeping. This is the first sentence of the blessing with which Aaron and his sons were to bless the Israelites. It spoke of protection and favor, and I bless you, _____, to rejoice in the kind hand of the One who watches over you for good.

I bless you to live in the freedom of knowing that God's "got your back" even in hard times. And I bless you with sleep unhindered by anxiety and worry for God neither slumbers nor sleeps, so the night watches are His to protect, not yours.

The three-fold repetition of the Lord's name—Yahweh—reveals that God wanted His people to know, without a doubt, that He is the source of all their blessing. It did not come as a result of happenstance or their own ability to make things turn out well. I bless you, _____, to bestow all credit on the One who loves you and blesses you. Let your response to good always default to acclaim God as your supply.

The first blessing flows into the second: *"The Lord make His face shine upon you, and be gracious to you."* I encourage you to feel the warmth of God's smile upon your soul. I bless you with the intimate relationship with God that Moses had which resulted in his face aglow with the glory of God after spending time in His presence. And I bless you with grace-upon-grace as you live out the God-calling on your life with a rich supply of ALL you need.

The final portion of the blessing culminates in the ultimate reward: *"The Lord lift up His countenance upon you, and give you peace."* More than a feel-good ending, this proclaims the crescendo of blessing-upon-blessing to you. God looks with full-face favor and grants you His *shalom* peace.

_____, you have been granted wholeness and healing that has no earthly comparison. God's blessing on you in Christ marks you as His own, and He is completely true to His promise to unde-niably bless you. In the name of Yahweh, you have been blessed for all time throughout eternity with the name of Christ emblazoned on your soul for all the heavenly host to see. You are blessed indeed.

Notes (anything I need to do/think differently/consider who needs to hear this, etc.):

BLESSING 30: KIND WORKMANSHIP

_____, hear the Word of God in Ephesians 2:8-10 with ears ready to listen and obey. *"For by grace you have been saved through faith, and that not of yourselves; it is the gift of God, not of works, lest anyone should boast. For we are His workmanship, created in Christ Jesus for good works, which God prepared beforehand that we should walk in them."*

You have been granted grace beyond all measure of understanding. In the verse prior to this passage, God says that He showed the *"exceeding riches of His grace in His kindness toward us in Christ Jesus."*

I bless you, _____, with an enlarged capacity to treasure and tell of God's kindness toward you. His gift is irrevocable and your rescue from the clutches of the enemy is a gift in more than every sense of the word. Undeserved. Unattainable by you. Inconceivable. And utterly, incredibly bestowed in glorious wonder upon you as a bountiful blessing of monumental proportion.

I bless you, _____, to soak in the astonishment of the gospel often and with unabashed delight. I bless you to respond to God with fresh excitement and escalating thankfulness. And I bless you to be saturated with God-wonder and God-worship.

While your works played no part in God delivering you from sin and death, God has created you with works in mind. You are His *"workmanship"*—His creation in Christ—and He has crafted you specifically for an admirable purpose.

I bless you, _____, to rejoice that God's hand in creating you is for good. The works that He has for you were prepared individually for you and long before you were even born. I bless you to view your life from the Creator's perspective and determine to display His creative hand of glory in the giftings you have been granted.

I bless you to draw upon every ounce of faith in God as you *walk out* your calling; and, whether it proves intensely rewarding, incredibly frustrating or a mixture of the two, I bless you to find great satisfaction as you call upon the Spirit's power to sustain you with great joy. I bless you, _____, to so shine with God's greatness, glory and grace that your reflection of Christ will cause others to gaze in astonishment at the God who has graced you with rich kindness for His glory.

I bless you in the name of the Father, who chose you; in the name of the Son, whose ransom paid for your life to be a work of honor and blessing for His Father; and in the name of the Spirit, whose indwelling presence gives you the impetus to live for Christ and to bring living color to the Creator's design for your life of good works.

Notes (anything I need to do/think differently/consider who needs to hear this, etc.):

BLESSING 31: BOLD BREAKTHROUGH

_____, listen to the following words inscribed in Scripture in the fourth chapter of Acts: *"Now, Lord, look on their threats, and grant to Your servants that with all boldness they may speak Your word, by stretching out Your hand to heal, and that signs and wonders may be done through the name of Your holy Servant Jesus"* (v. 29-30). This prayer by Peter and John and the early church believers was, as described in verse 24, raised to God *"with one accord."*

The believers were not only gathered together physically, but they were also of one mind and heart and were in complete agreement in their petition that Peter and John—who had been imprisoned and warned by the Jewish leaders to never again mention the name of Jesus—would continue to do what they had told the rulers: *"We cannot but speak the things which we have seen and heard"* (v. 20).

I bless you, _____, to be blessed with a host of believers who will join you in unity praying for answers that defy human wisdom and human intervention. I bless you to connect with them in like-hearted passion to beseech God to break through insurmountable barriers. And I bless you to implore with a singular voice of praise that proclaims the preeminence of Christ and His power to eradicate enemy plans.

This band of believers was downright determined in their appeal and devotion, fully convinced that God would answer NOW. I bless you, _____, to so pray in accordance with the will and the power of the Spirit that you target the bulls-eye every time.

I bless you to be so intentional in your requests and your acclaim of God that the words of your tongue are the translated utterances of the Spirit who *"intercedes and pleads [before God] in behalf of the saints according to and in harmony with God's will"* (Romans 8:27b, Amplified Bible). And I bless you to not hold back in requesting God to confirm the speaking of His Word with His hand of healing and His miracles and wonders wholly accomplished through the name of Jesus.

This "one accord" unified and undivided praying produced a NOW response from God, as *"the place where they were assembled together was shaken; and they were all filled with the Holy Spirit, and they spoke the word of God with boldness"* (Acts 4:31).

I bless you, _____, to experience similar remarkable prayer responses. These early church believers encountered an external, internal and then another external answer, as God reacted radically in three ways. He dramatically demonstrated His power by shaking the ground, then saturating them with His Spirit which empowered them to do exactly what they asked—speak boldly— with His power providing their stamp of approval.

I bless you, _____, to seek God with all the passion of the gathered believers in Acts 4 so that you will be granted precisely what you ask. I bless you to break through enemy territory with boldness that bespeaks of God's glory and the Spirit's enabling in the name above all names—JESUS!

And I bless you to shout of God's greatness with a ground-shaking, groundswell of perpetual praise, for God responds to the praise and prayers of His people with a fanfare none can match.

I bless you in the MATCHLESS name of Jesus, whose lifeblood was plundered on our behalf so that we can rejoice, praise and petition in unity for God's power to be unleashed on earth as it is in heaven.

Notes (anything I need to do/think differently/consider who needs to hear this, etc.):

Testimonial/feedback: "At times, the Lord has prompted me to recycle the blessings to bless other. They have been read over Lainey and Sarah being sent out on a mission trip to Haiti with the USC football team; spoken to our church staff for encouragement; used to bless my grown daughter in times of trials; spoken over members of our Uganda missions teams here while in training; read to the Ugandans themselves; and used to bless the dear godly men and women in my Lifegroup and Monday morning prayer group. All have been deeply touched to hear the truth of the living word spoken over them."

BLESSING 32: LISTENING AND LIVING!

_____, the following words were written by James in verses 19 and 20 of chapter one: *"So then, my beloved brethren, let every man be swift to hear, slow to speak, slow to wrath; for the wrath of man does not produce the righteousness of God."* James speaks much more about the tongue in chapter three, but here he introduces the connection between how we listen, how we speak and the propensity to anger, so we would be wise to pay attention.

I bless you, _____, with the desire to glean all that Scripture offers, for its truth leads to life.

While this wisdom is profound, it comes on the heels of other insight, for the words, *"So then, my beloved brethren"* beg the question: "What precedes *so then* that leads to this wisdom?" Why follow James' directive? In context, James is detailing the truth that trials WILL come, and we are blessed if we endure and not be enticed to sin.

We are, after all, the FIRSTFRUITS of God—completely delivered to be set apart for God's glory! So this "listen quickly, speak intentionally and hold off on anger" wisdom is key to prevailing in trials.

I bless you, _____, to take this three-fold *"triumphing-in-trials"* incentive to heart. I bless you to choose to put this into practice BEFORE trials come. And I bless you to practice until it becomes so ingrained in your soul and spirit that trials will only sharpen your resolve to see that your heart and your tongue are in sync with God's best.

The first part of the admonition? *"Let every man be swift to hear."* Hearing entails more than being quiet while someone else has their say. It encompasses vastly more than merely listening to words as they are read from Scripture.

So I bless you, _____, to be attentive to both God and man. As you hearken your heart to hear what God speaks to you in your study of His Word and in your quiet time, you will be refreshed and ready to listen to people, even those who are trying. I bless you to attend to God's voice and to listen to what He says. In turn, then, I bless you to filter what others say through what you know God requires of you and how He empowers you to withstand temptation.

"Be slow to speak" is the perfect complement to the first part of this James 1:19-20 wisdom, for intentional listening must be linked to intentional speaking. I bless you, _____, to hold off on an immediate reply so that you spend time discerning the spiritual warfare at play instead of trying to formulate a rebuttal in your own mind that will cause the enemy to rejoice.

James knows that God requires more than adherence to keeping quiet. So I bless you, _____, to keep your tongue in check with the Holy Spirit as you speak so that the words of your mouth and the meditation of your heart are in accordance with Psalm 19:14 and are acceptable in the sight of our Lord, our Rock and our Redeemer. And I bless you with Colossians 4:6 wisdom: *"Let your speech always be with grace, seasoned with salt, that you may know how you ought to answer each one."*

Following God's directions for listening and speaking make the third directive much easier: *"Be slow to wrath, for the wrath of man does not produce the righteousness of God."* As you choose to listen and speak with God's intent and heart at your very core, I bless you, _____, with a compassion that keeps anger far from crouching at your door.

I bless you to not mull the conversation over and over in your mind so that the victory gives way to latent animosity. I bless you to settle on patience over pride, peace over petulance and blessing over blasting. Then you will overcome the testing and trial!

I bless you in the name of God Almighty, who triumphs over the foe victoriously and empowers you through His Spirit to control your heart, mind and tongue so that His Word will prevail over your life in great power and with His great pleasure!

Notes (anything I need to do/think differently/consider who needs to hear this, etc.):

BLESSING 33: IMMEASURABLE LOVE

I bless you, _____, with the words of the Lord written in John 8:29. Jesus spoke of His relationship with the Father—and their intimacy is absolutely critical to success in any and every area of a Christ-follower's life. Jesus said, *"He who sent Me is with Me. The Father has not left Me alone, for I always do those things that please Him."*

I bless you, _____, to live completely cloaked in the Father's affection, love and protection. I bless you to be so incredibly entwined with the Father's heart that you will never feel abandoned or alone, even in the most trying of times. And I encourage you to please the Lord extravagantly as you sojourn through life, always attentive to the Father's *pleasure of* and *love for* you.

Out of that overflow, _____, you will be empowered to be a life-giver and a love-giver. According to Luke 6:37-8: *"Do not judge, and you will not be judged. Do not condemn, and you will not be condemned. Forgive, and you will be forgiven. Give, and it will be given to you. A good measure, pressed down, shaken together and running over, will be poured into your lap. For with the measure you use, it will be measured to you"* (NIV).

So, I bless you, _____, to draw from the vast reservoir of the Father's heart, the Son's lifeblood and the Spirit's power—and pour life and love into all those your life will touch. I bless you with not only a double portion, but instead a multiplied measure of the Spirit's fruit to invest.

I bless you with lavish love, generous joy, potent peace, a prevalence of patience, endless kindness, forever faithfulness, tender gentleness, gratifying goodness and superabundant self-control.

In Proverbs 11:25, it says: *"The generous soul will be made rich, and he who waters will also be watered himself."* That verse characterizes you, _____, and so I bless you—as you give—to receive more to restore you and to replenish your supply to bestow on others.

I bless you with an open heart and open hands. I bless you with a Spirit-filling, Father-pleasing, Son-rejoicing life on brilliant display for all to see.

I bless you in the name of the Father, whose love for you drew you to Himself; in the name of the Son, whose blood-spilt sacrifice called you out of darkness into light; and in the name of the Spirit, whose presence catapults you into a *"no regrets"* life of immeasurable giving and receiving! You are blessed indeed!

Notes (anything I need to do/think differently/consider who needs to hear this, etc.):

BLESSING 34: MIRRORED GLORY

I bless you, _____, with the words of encouragement in 2 Corinthians 3:16-18: *"Nevertheless when one turns to the Lord, the veil is taken away. Now the Lord is the Spirit; and where the Spirit of the Lord is, there is liberty. But we all, with unveiled face, beholding as in a mirror the glory of the Lord, are being transformed into the same image from glory to glory, just as by the Spirit of the Lord."*

You are an unveiled masterpiece, crafted by God and sculpted by the Spirit. I bless you, _____, to peer beyond the physical to gaze on the spiritual manifestation of God's workmanship of you, for you are ablaze with reflected glory that stops the enemy in his tracks and draws believers into the light of the truth.

I bless you, _____, to behold in your spirit the living God who makes all things new and to look so intently into His face that glory streams from your innermost being. I bless you with unmistakably glorious life that stares down the death-gaze of the enemy. And I bless you with the Spirit of the living God powerfully breathing with you and through you the Father's heart and the Son's authority.

"Where the Spirit of the Lord is, there is liberty" (2 Cor. 3:17). The Spirit is the ink of the new covenant, and He writes on tablets of flesh, that is, of the heart (2 Cor. 3:3).

I bless you, _____, to open hearts with the razor-sharp precision of the Word and plunder enemy territory by rewriting scripts with the Spirit's hand. I bless you to edit the enemy's scribbles of deprivation, disaster and destruction and instead pen the Spirit's words of inspiration, encouragement and energetic life.

And I bless you to watch your own story unfold in majestic wonder as you selflessly weave the Spirit's life into the stories of others.

"Therefore," the Apostle Paul continues in the next verse in 2 Corinthians, *"since we have this ministry, as we have received mercy, we do not lose heart"* (4:1). The Lord, in His mercy, has made you trustworthy in the undertaking of ministry to others, and He encourages you to not lose heart. Not once—but twice—in this chapter does Paul say the exact same words about not losing heart.

So I bless you, _____, to not lose heart, as God promises that you have received mercy and that your *"inward man"* is being renewed daily. I bless you to bask in God's marvelous mercy and His restorative renewal. I bless you to look not at the temporary but to cast your eyes and your heart upon the eternal so that the glory of the Lord is your forward vision and your rear guard.

I bless you, _____, in the radiant light of the living God whose glory transforms you into the likeness and image of Jesus; whose glory outshines every obstacle you'll ever face; and whose glory breathes resurrection life into your weary heart.

Notes (anything I need to do/think differently/consider who needs to hear this, etc.):

Blessing 35: Multiplied Grace and Peace

_____, listen to the Word of God written in 2 Peter 1:2: *"Grace and peace be multiplied to you in the knowledge of God and of Jesus our Lord."* Your life is—and will be—characterized by grace and peace in great measure, because you KNOW God, and your life reflects a heart ransomed by Jesus. Multiplied grace and peace, then, are the outpouring of a life of intimacy whereby you have worshipped, listened, conversed, wrestled and been captured by the Father's heart for you.

I bless you, _____, with a life bursting full of grace and peace that trumps human wisdom and natural intervention. I bless you with persevering when the odds seem stacked against you, because you trust the One who coaches you. And I bless you with playing God's way with grace and peace being both the defensive and offensive strategy to lead you to triumph over the enemy.

For God knows that a victorious life in Him requires grace and peace, as His *"divine power has given to us all things that pertain to life and godliness, through the knowledge of Him who called us by glory and virtue, by which have been given to us exceedingly great and precious promises, that through these you may be partakers of the divine nature, having escaped the corruption that is in the world through lust"* (2 Peter 2:2-4).

Godliness can only flourish in a grace-saturated and peace-infused atmosphere. You, _____, have taken spiritual ground with calculated steps that embrace God's gifts of grace and peace and all that you need to advance. I bless you with walking and warring in the brilliance of God's great glory and excellence. I bless your person and your potential with receiving and appropriating all the gifts God has bestowed on you so that your life will rebound with vigor and victory.

_____, as you traverse through life with God's favor as your covering, I bless your vision to encompass the grandeur of God's exceedingly great and precious promises. I bless you to prioritize your days with His promises in as clear a view as if God had emblazoned them in precise detail on a winning game plan.

You are a keeper and a conduit of God's promises, and I bless you as you shine God's bias on others, snatching them from a world of destruction and hurt and inviting them to partake of God's goodness.

And, as praise to God permeates your heart for all He has given you and promised to you, I bless you, _____, to experience the manifest presence of the One who covenants with you for good. I bless you to tilt your ear to hear His accolades, and I bless you to reverberate His heart back to Him, with a standing ovation that brings joy to all of heaven as they join you in a crescendo of glory-rising praise to our awesome God!

I bless you in the name of Yeshua, who took on human flesh so that you can stand confidently in the favor of His light with hands open to receive multiplied grace and peace that boosts faith, forfeits fear and fuels life! You have been blessed to be a blessing!

Notes (anything I need to do/think differently/consider who needs to hear this, etc.):

Blessing 36: Heart Attitude

_____, the following verses from God's Word are a lifeline of wisdom. Listen to these two verses from Ephesians 4:31-32: *"Let all bitterness, wrath, anger, clamor, and evil speaking be put away from you, with all malice. And be kind to one another, tenderhearted, forgiving one another, even as God in Christ forgave you."*

These verses weren't written to unregenerate people but to the believers at Ephesus. The Apostle Paul, through inspiration of the Spirit, inscribed these words so that all generations—beginning with those who lived soon after Christ's resurrection—would be encouraged to follow God's heart in their thoughts, in their speech and in their actions. So I bless you, _____, to view these two verses as God's special wisdom to you.

Paul details six things to put away and three things *"to be."* Of the six to not allow in, four can infect the heart. _____, I bless you with exceptional discernment and awareness of the enemy's intent to tempt with these four: bitterness, wrath, anger and malice.

I bless you to halt them before they enter, and I bless you to put distance between you and their mercenary attacks. Once they are allowed access, they will eventually erupt in clamor—which refers to loud quarreling—and also to evil speaking. Therefore, I bless you to give no place or voice to these six, as they will only undermine your love for others.

Instead, God offers His remedy. He encourages us to be kind, tenderhearted and forgiving. I bless you, _____, with God's *instead* heart attitudes that will cancel the enemy's plans every time. I bless you to be incredibly intentional about how to be as well as what to exclude.

And since both begin with the heart, I bless you with a heart so immensely overtaken with love for Jesus that you will choose kindness over clamor, tenderness over temptations toward bitterness and anger, and forgiveness when the enemy wedges his way into any of your relationships.

I bless you to emulate Jesus and His sacrifice continually and compassionately. I bless you with grace in your heart and your speech so that *"no corrupt word will proceed out of your mouth, but only what is good for necessary edification, that it may impart grace to the hearers."*

And I bless you to *"not grieve the Holy Spirit of God, by whom you were sealed for the day of redemption"* (Ephesians 4:29-30). Remember that you are sealed by the Spirit to be a living, colorful, beautiful illustration of God's heart to a world in desperate need of the gospel. I bless you to literally and figuratively shout out the good news through your life.

_____, I bless you with a heart steadfast and immoveable, fully focused on and faithful to the One True God, in whose name I bless you to forever sing in word and heart and action:

"The steadfast love of the Lord never ceases,

His mercies never come to an end,

They are new every morning, new every morning

Great is Thy faithfulness (Oh Lord)

Great is Thy faithfulness."

Notes (anything I need to do/think differently/consider who needs to hear this, etc.):

"My dear friend Ruth called me and read this blessing to me one day, and I emailed this response to her later: 'This is PERFECT for all of the things I have been thinking about and processing this morning!!! I literally JUST sat down with my Bible study, and my phone beeped! Thank you so much for all you do to encourage me! I don't know if you truly know the impact you have in my life! I love how God works through our friends when we need to hear from Him the most!'"

BLESSING 37: DESTINATION: A NEW THING!

_____, listen to the following words inscribed in Scripture in Isaiah 43:19: *"Behold, I will do a new thing. Now it shall spring forth; shall you not know it? I will even make a road in the wilderness and rivers in the desert."* In context, Isaiah declares God's providential care for His people in the midst of captivity and trial and His overarching plan to bring His redemptive purposes to bear in their lives. As such, its message is timeless.

I bless you, _____, to lift your head and your heart to see with crystal-clear clarity what God is doing in your life. God is *always* up to something. As He draws you from glory to glory, I bless you to be aware of the nuances of His nearness. I bless you to sense His presence in the mundane and the mania of life.

And I bless you to not misconstrue His purposes and ways, which being *"not our ways"* can often be misunderstood.

This new thing that God is doing in your life is a path propelling you to a new destination and always directs you to experience more of Him, provided that you follow His leading. I bless you to not mistake the gateway and path for a roadblock. I bless you to enter the gate by way of thanksgiving, unlocking the potential for a grand entrance. And I bless you to perceive the path with eyes of faith and eyes locked with His.

The path is an essential ingredient of the new thing, and it can spring forth suddenly, often taking you by surprise, catapulting you from the normal to a *"new normal."* Ask God to illumine your route with His wisdom, asking in faith without doubting, for then it will be granted to you in rich supply. I bless you to heed His wisdom so that your steps are sure and He becomes your focal point, not the wilderness that the road winds through.

Rejoice that He maneuvers you by way of a road, not dumping you into the wilderness alone—devoid of direction.

I bless you, _____, to drink deeply at the river that He makes in the desert just for you. Stop and refill with the Spirit constantly. It will not lengthen your journey but lighten it. Refresh yourself with His Word, with songs of joy and with the fellowship of the saints.

I bless you to resolve to walk steadfastly and to glory in the light, the road and the water He bestows. Your sojourning will strengthen and equip you to enter into the new land. I bless you to *"dwell in the land, and feed on His faithfulness"* (Psalm 37:3b) until He does another new thing that will call you onward and upward.

I bless you, _____, in the name of Jesus of Nazareth, whose journey to earth bought you a new lease of abundant life in the here and now and a forever inheritance of joy in heaven with Him.

Notes (anything I need to do/think differently/consider who needs to hear this, etc.):

Testimonial/feedback: "I was read 'Destination: A New Thing' out loud at a very painful time in my life. The comfort of Isaiah 43:19 was from the Lord right when my heart needed encouragement. As I have been on my wilderness journey, this blessing helped me to be thankful and give God the glory.

"This blessing helped me to receive His path and draw me to a deeper and rich relationship as I savor His presence, bringing peace to my spirit. Yes, I'm headed to the new land which I look forward to dwell in.

"Thank you for writing this moving piece. My copy of 'Destination: A New Thing' is tattered and has been a special gift from the Lord."

BLESSING 38: INTRUDERS BEGONE!

_____, listen to the following words inscribed in Scripture in Ephesians 6:12-13: *"For we do not wrestle against flesh and blood, but against principalities, against powers, against the rulers of the darkness of this age, against spiritual hosts of wickedness in the heavenly places. Therefore take up the whole armor of God, that you may be able to withstand in the evil day, and having done all, to stand."*

The Apostle Paul warns of an enemy who does not use worldly warfare. The combat armor God chooses for His children protects with truth, righteousness, salvation, the gospel of peace and with faith; and it overcomes the adversary with the Word and with prayer in the Spirit.

I bless you, _____, to view every earthly battle with spiritual eyes. I bless you to contend with no physical person but with the powers behind the afflicted persona. And I bless you to persist against the thoughts that the opponent plants with deceitful seeds of poison. They are meant to intrude upon your peace and life. Battle instead with God's chosen arsenal of weaponry.

_____, where doubt has crept in, I bless you to instead open your heart to embrace hope. For *"hope does not disappoint, because the love of God has been poured out in our hearts by the Holy Spirit who was given to us"* (Romans 5:5).

When fear comes calling, I bless you to instead entertain the love of the Lord, for *"there is no fear in love; but perfect love casts out fear, because fear involves torment"* (1 John 4:18a).

When faltering in the midst of trials is encouraged by the enemy, I bless you to instead choose to step out in faith, for *"faith is the substance of things hoped for, the evidence of things not seen"* (Hebrews 11:1) and *"Count it all joy when you fall into various trials, knowing that the testing of your faith produces patience. But let patience have its perfect work, that you may be perfect and complete, lacking nothing"* (James 1:2-4).

Instead of being a victim, you are *"more than a conqueror through Him who loved us"* (Romans 8:37).

Instead of rejected and abandoned, you are ransomed and adopted, for *"when the fullness of the time had come, God sent forth His Son, born of a woman, born under the law, to redeem those who were under the law, that we might receive the adoption as sons. And because you are sons, God has sent forth the Spirit of His Son into your hearts, crying out, 'Abba, Father'"* (Galatians 4:4-6).

Instead of deeming yourself powerless, God wants you to be convinced of *"the exceeding greatness of His power toward us who believe, according to the working of His mighty power which He worked in Christ when He raised Him from the dead and seated Him at His right hand in the heavenly places, far above all principality and power and might and dominion, and every name that is named, not only in this age but also in that which is to come"* (Ephesians 1:19-21).

Therefore, I bless you, _____, to joust with the "instead" weapons God has granted you so that you will triumph over the enemy's tactics.

I bless you in the name of Jesus, the Lion of Judah, whose power trumps the lion who seeks whom he may devour, for the Lion of Judah reigns forever and ever, world without end, Amen.

Notes (anything I need to do/think differently/consider who needs to hear this, etc.):

Testimonial/feedback: "I was given this blessing when I was directly in the midst of a major trial. It helped me reorient how I was thinking and feeling and helped me to not lash out at the people around me. I was thankful that I could read it over and over, and I found that when I did that (even reading it aloud on occasion), my attitude changed."

BLESSING 39: LIVES CHANGED!

_____, listen to the following words the Apostle Paul penned nearly two-thousand years ago under the inspiration of the Holy Spirit: *"He has delivered us from the power of darkness and conveyed us into the kingdom of the Son of His love"* (Colossians 1:13). This verse—a simply stated twenty-one words—is charged with meaning for a lifetime. You are not your own and never have been. You were held captive by the power of darkness. Controlled, manipulated and deceived.

But you have been delivered. You have been freed, liberated, acquitted, discharged, emancipated, loosed, released, rescued, saved and unshackled from the enemy's clutches! Ransomed from darkness and transported to a new kingdom.

I bless you, _____, to remember and recount your ransoming often. I bless you to let praise rain down on and reign in your heart as you consider the incredible transformation of your life: body, soul and spirit! You have been bought and brought from darkness to light, from death to life and from disgrace to honor.

Your deliverance to the kingdom of Jesus is for a distinct purpose. Therefore, you are called to live in the power of the Spirit daily, testifying to the world that you live under the rule and headship of Christ Jesus. Your old ruler will try you and test your allegiance.

He will plant doubts and question your current situation and your King.

I bless you, _____, to not be surprised by the trials that come your way. I bless you to scrutinize them in light of your place in the kingdom of Light as a light-bearer, not a shadow-caster. And I bless you to look deep into the eyes of the Son of God's love and behold the marvelous redemptive gaze that transfigures the trivial by way of majesty.

Oh, to know, really know, that you are called to be a *Life Changer.* You are not on hold. Your prayers can avail much (James 5:16b). Your encouragement may be just the words necessary to lift the spirit of a friend. The giving of your time, talents and treasure may precipitate a God movement that will bring a Colossians 1:13 avalanche into a nation of those held captive by the power of darkness. So I bless you, _____, to know *"the love of Christ which passes knowledge that you may be filled up to all the fullness of God"* (Ephesians 3:19).

I bless you, _____, in the name of the Son of His love, who laid down His very life so that you could be raised up victorious in this life and the next, world without end, Amen.

Notes (anything I need to do/think differently/consider who needs to hear this, etc.):

BLESSING 40: NEW SONG

_____, God is a master at melody. Listen to His words written in Psalm 40:1-3: *"I waited patiently for the Lord; and He inclined to me, and heard my cry. He also brought me up out of a horrible pit, out of the miry clay, and set my feet upon a rock, and established my steps. He has put a new song in my mouth—praise to our God. Many will see it and fear, and will trust in the Lord."*

Sometimes, we just need to know that our cries are heard. God hears. And He not only hears, He first inclines His ear to your very cry, which means that He *"feels willing or favorably disposed"* toward you. I bless you, _____, to let this truth sink deep into your understanding and saturate your heart. God is favorably inclined toward you. God leans toward you. God is for you.

God also responds to your cry with action. He acts even when you're in a pit, perhaps one of horrible dimensions. He does what man cannot do. He orchestrates a recovery that causes you to rise up and out of that abyss. He *establishes* your steps. He inaugurates and sets into motion a solid, trustworthy walk, for you have been called to follow His leading and His footsteps.

_____, God's declaration over your life is a masterpiece of praise. He replaces your cry with a song, a new song of praise. You might be in a place where you're asking for an extra lyric that will brighten your day. You could be clamoring for a change in the refrain that you sing. Maybe you'd like to belt out a different harmony. GOD desires to bless you with an entire *new song* of praise.

I bless you, _____, to still your heart so as to incline it toward the GIVER of all good gifts. I bless you to listen with expectancy and believe that God has a new song for you to sing. I bless you with joyous wonder and attuned heart as He sings your song over you.

And I bless your heart and mind and soul to erupt in glorious praise to the One who *"will rejoice over you with gladness."* For He will indeed *"quiet you with His love. He will rejoice over you with singing"* (Zephaniah 3:17).

I bless you, _____, in the name of Jesus Christ, the Lamb of God, who will one day take the scroll, and the four living creatures and the twenty-four elders will fall down before Him. And they will sing a new song, saying: *"You are worthy to take the scroll, and to open its seals; for You were slain, and have redeemed us to God by Your blood out of every tribe and tongue and people and nation, and have made us kings and priests to our God; and we shall reign on the earth"* (Revelation 5:8-10).

Blessed be the name of the LORD! Sing with wild abandon, dearly beloved child of God, the new song He gives you to sing!

Notes (anything I need to do/think differently/consider who needs to hear this, etc.):

Testimonial/feedback: "Receiving this blessing not only confirmed the healing God was doing in my heart, but also gave me the freedom and excitement to be brave to sing the 'New Song' God had spoken over me both through His word, my small group, and my intimate times with Him."

BLESSING 41: TAKE GOD AT HIS WORD!

_____, what if today you make a choice to take God at His Word? Not just mental assent. Not meditation that stops short of movement. But instead you choose real, true Word-of-God motivated and Word-of-God inspired change. *"For the word of God is living and powerful, and sharper than any two-edged sword, piercing even to the division of soul and spirit, and of joints and marrow, and is a discerner of the thoughts and intents of the heart"* (Hebrews 4:12).

Do you believe it?

I bless you, _____, to allow the Word of God to break into your today. To do so, you will have to be intentionally relentless in your faith walk. *"For faith comes by hearing, and hearing by the word of God"* (Romans 10:17). You will have to proceed with persistence and ruthless resolve. I bless your ears to hear God's truth and transcribe it on your heart so that the eyes of your heart gaze intently on the face of Jesus.

What then will your day be like?

You will choose God's peace over fear. Your knees will drop to the ground in prayer and petition as you speak out thankfulness to and for your God who promises His peace.

It will settle your heart.

You will forfeit revenge and determine to forgive.

You will rejoice in God's love when rejection rears its head.

You will pray for your friends AND your enemies.

You will bless rather than curse.

You will choose hope over disappointment.

You will give thanks, and not just for your meals. You will choose thanksgiving as a life-line.

You will seek God's wisdom FIRST.

You will choose the Holy Spirit as your paramount Counselor, Teacher, and Comforter.

Instead of speaking half-truths or aligning yourself with a lie, you will speak the truth, always harmonizing it with love.

You will choose to love…period.

Realize that what you see may be displayed starkly different than what God's Word proclaims. Where they differ, _____, I urge you to stand on the Word of God over your physical sight, your conflicting emotions and your vision of the future. God will make a way as you submit your will to His Word and follow His way.

_____, I bless you to take God at His Word every minute of every day. For then you will be blessed beyond anything you can envision with increasing and overarching love, joy, peace, patience, kindness, goodness, gentleness and self-control. Oh, the incredible delight of taking God at His Word!

I bless you in the name of *"the God and Father of our Lord Jesus Christ, who has blessed us with every spiritual blessing in the heavenly places in Christ, just as He chose us in Him before the foundation of the world, that we should be holy and without blame before Him in love"* (Ephesians 1:3-4). Take God at His Word and really live!

Philippians 4:8-9; Matthew 6:14; Ephesians 3:17-19; Matthew 5:44; Romans 12:14; Romans 5:5; 1 Thessalonians 5:18; Matthew 6:33; John 14:26; Ephesians 4:15; 1 Corinthians 13; Galatians 5:22

Notes (anything I need to do/think differently/consider who needs to hear this, etc.):

Testimonial/feedback: "The truth in this blessing has impacted my life tremendously. More than anything, I have learned to rest in God's love for me and to bless others and pray for them and to forgive readily. When I do that, my heart changes—toward myself and toward others. It's as if I understand God's heart better, and that's a beautiful gift."

BLESSING 42: BUT GOD

_____, you always have the last, final, triumphant word in every situation, for God is in you, the hope of glory. For once you were in darkness. BUT God, rich in mercy, ransomed you from a life of desolation and an eternity in hell. He has given you everything you need to live this life in godliness (2 Peter 1:3).

I bless you, _____, with a God perspective that turns the tables on every enemy attempt to push you over the edge. I bless you to stand fast, immoveable, ever abounding in the work of the Lord. I bless you to resolutely respond to feelings and circumstances with a "But God" affirmation.

You might feel weary and ready to give up, but God is *"your strength, your personal bravery, your invincible army. He makes your feet like hinds' feet and will make you to walk [not to stand still in terror, but to walk] and make [spiritual] progress upon your high places [of trouble, suffering, or responsibility]"* (Habakkuk 3:19, AMP).

You might find your situation worrisome, but God's peace will guard your heart and mind in Christ Jesus as you come to Him with your supplications in an attitude of thanksgiving.

You might be experiencing weakness, but God's strength is made perfect in human weakness (2 Cor. 12:9a). _____, I exhort you to powerfully proclaim with the Apostle Paul the words in 2 Corinthians 4:7-10: *"But we have this treasure in earthen vessels, that the excellence of the power may be of God and not of us. We are hard-pressed on every side, yet not crushed; we are perplexed, but not in despair; persecuted, but not forsaken; struck down, but not destroyed— always carrying about in the body the dying of the Lord Jesus, that the life of Jesus also may be manifested in our body."*

I bless you, _____, in the name of Jesus of Nazareth, who lives in you with UNENDING LIFE that overtakes every objection with His unmistakable power and presence!

Notes (anything I need to do/think differently/consider who needs to hear this, etc.):

Testimonial/feedback: "As we go through life and people we know are going through trials, one way to encourage others is to read or send a blessing to them. It is amazing how a specific blessing can be just what will speak to someone's heart. The Lord's love for us comes from words He has given to minister in a way that only He can do. Sometimes we don't know what to say to a loved one or a stranger, and that's what is so wonderful about all of the blessings in this book. I suggest praying about which one to read or send to someone you want to encourage. In my own life, a blessing prayed over me has spoken the Lord's love for me in a way that is hard to describe. It is such an encouragement when words touch you in such a tender and uplifting manner."

BLESSING 43: FRUIT BEARER

_____, the Lord is your Shepherd; you shall not want. He makes you to lie down in green pastures; He leads you beside the still waters. He restores your soul, and He leads you in the paths of righteousness for His name's sake (Psalm 23:1-3). You are God's. Period. He watches over your comings and goings, intercepts your thoughts and calms your fears.

I bless you to rest in the knowledge that He is your KEEPER. He keeps watch. He keeps your tears in His bottle. He keeps your heart steadfast. He keeps the enemy on a leash. He keeps guard.

His love never changes. _____, I bless you to see His love in its complexity and its purity, in its movement and its solidity, in the way He speaks and sings over you and to you, and in the way He brings brilliance and clarity into every shadow.

"For you died, and your life is hidden with Christ in God" (Colossians 3:3). You are no longer alive to sin, no longer alive to the passions of the world. You have died to the self-propagating, self-perpetuating life of the old man and you are now ALIVE to the purposes and plans of the LIVING GOD! For you have died to be resurrected to a LIVING HOPE.

I bless you, _____, with renewed vision of resurrected life in Christ. I bless you to dance again, this time as one locked in an embrace with Christ, whose power and love pours invigoration into bodies of flesh. I bless you to respond to His invitation of still-water leading and soul restoration with joy and anticipation that springs from a heart fully engaged with the Shepherd.

It's not a dichotomy to both "lie down" and "dance," for He is a God of creation and calmness, composure and drama, excitement and empathy. The womb holds the child in a place of nourishing, hidden creative life that leads to breakthrough expression of God-breathed individuality.

You, _____, will be fruitful. Nothing is hidden from the Lord. Your hidden life in Christ is being birthed through the hands of the One who guides your life and heart. He calls you to *"walk by faith, not by sight"* (2 Cor. 5:7), so I bless you to be a faith-walker, not a sight-seeker.

I bless you to covenant with God to trust. I bless you to trust in God. I bless you to trust in God's timing. I bless you to trust in God's intention. I bless you to trust in God's heart for you. I bless you to trust in God's birthing process. I bless you to trust in God's hiddenness and in His open approval of you.

I bless you to trust in God's love. I bless you to trust in God's jubilant joy. I bless you trust in God's perfect peace. I bless you to trust in God's rich patience. I bless you to trust in God's tender kindness. I bless you to trust in God's goodness. I bless you to trust in God's faithfulness. I bless you to trust in God's gentleness, and I bless you to trust in God's control (Galatians 5:22-23).

I bless you, _____, in the name of Jesus Christ, for you are His. You are completely hidden with Him and your life shines with the intense glory of His presence in the duress and the delight of life. You are unconditionally His.

Notes (anything I need to do/think differently/consider who needs to hear this, etc.):

Testimonial/feedback: "*Incredible how this one hit the nail on the head for me in regards to trust. When these words were spoken over me with conviction, I realized that God was calling me to a deeper level of trust. I'm ready to rethink and give up the superficial way I've 'trusted' in God.*"

Blessing 44: Obstacle in Place

_____, each morning is a gift from God. God gives life and breath and gifts you with new mercies every morning. You have a choice every morning when you wake up. You can choose to arise and depend upon the Lord, causing you to bask in the sunlight/dance in the rain, or you can choose to bemoan the heat and scowl at the clouds. Your predisposition will set the mood and the course for that day.

I bless you, _____, to sing aloud with the psalmist David in Psalm 59:16: *"But I will sing of Your power. Yes, I will sing aloud of Your mercy in the morning; for You have been my defense and refuge in the day of my trouble."* David was hiding from the men Saul sent to kill him when he penned this song. His choice was to not let the circumstances set the tone for his day. Instead he sung loudly of God's mercies and His power.

God is greater, and His power proclaims victory over what threatens you. His mercy holds the enemy at bay no matter how cleverly your adversary protests otherwise. I bless your praise of Yahweh to drown out the sly suggestions and willful woes of your opponent. You do not have to give ear to his whispered questions. You can preempt his voice with praise to the One who has wooed you, called you and strengthens you to withstand all temptation.

You will face obstacles. You live in enemy territory. This world is not yours, BUT you have kingdom authority to oppose every blockade without fear. You can walk in love and power, for God has not given you a spirit of fear, but of love and power and a sound mind. No matter how large that obstacle looms, you can put it in its place. God has granted you abundant life, so I bless you to choose LIFE, real living. The enemy may throw despair at you, but you can dodge it.

As you eye that obstacle, I bless you, _____, to superimpose the I AM over your hardship and see how it shrinks before your very eyes. Walk out your day with the God-view that substitutes wisdom for folly, rejoicing for complaining, Christ-confidence for fear, God-dependence for weakness—and laughter and joy for despair.

Psalm 139: 9-10 states: *"If I take the wings of the morning, and dwell in the uttermost parts of the sea, even there Your hand shall lead me, and Your right hand shall hold me."* You, _____, are not alone. I bless you to choose wisely and trust in God who never leaves you and never forsakes you. It's your choice. Believe Him and watch your obstacle find its place as a completely surmountable trial used by God to shape your character for your good and for His glory.

I bless you in the name of Jesus Christ, who, according to Revelation 22:16 says of Himself: *"I am the Root and the Offspring of David, the Bright and Morning Star."* May you, _____, awake every morning with a heart of love for the Bright and Morning Star who counters every darkness in your life with His glorious presence and majestic might.

Notes (anything I need to do/think differently/consider who needs to hear this, etc.):

BLESSING 45: LOOK ON UP!

Has anything gotten you down lately? It just may be that you have many circumstances to depress you; however, _____, it is not God's intent nor is it His plan for you to sink.

I bless you to take special note of the words written in Psalm 3: 3-4: *"But You, O Lord, are a shield for me, my glory and the One who lifts up my head. I cried to the Lord with my voice, and He heard me from His holy hill. Selah."* God is your stalwart shield, He is your glory and alone brings light to your life, and He is the One who can and does lift your head. I bless you to rise above the challenges of and the clamor in your life.

Unless your head is bowed low in worship and/or prayer, a lowered head usually denotes difficulty and depression. _____, I encourage you to live a life of light in the Lord, whereby your eyes and heart are desperate for God, not desperate over your circumstances. I bless you to consciously move your eyes upward, allowing your heart to beat in rhythm with the Lord's steadfast heart for you.

His resonant, booming heart drowns out all blasts of anxiety and despondency. I bless you to hear His voice crowd out all others! Cry out to the Lord with your voice. He hears and responds!

Don't miss the conclusion of Psalm 3:4. It ends with the word *"se-lah."* The Hebrew words from which *"selah"* is rendered encompass the meanings of praise, lift up and pause. Many believe it is a musical direction to the singers and/or instrumentalists who performed the Psalms, which was the hymnbook of the Israelites. Each time *"selah"* appears in a psalm, the musicians paused, either to take a breath, or to sing a cappella or let the instruments play alone. Perhaps they were pausing to praise God—about whom the song was speaking—maybe even lifting their hands in worship. This would encompass all these meanings—praise, lift up, and pause.

How fitting that this verse which speaks of God being the One who lifts your head and hears your cry ends with the *"selah"* directive to pause, lift up and praise.

I bless you, _____, to respond to every down moment with a lament to God who hearkens to hear your cry and to raise your head and your heart to behold Him. I bless you with *"selah"* comebacks that glorify Jesus. And I bless your position to always be one of a worshipper, head bent in worship and a heart lifted in praise.

I bless you, _____, in the name of the Most High God whom David lauded in Psalm 66:4: *"All the earth bows down to You; they sing praise to You, they sing praise to Your name." Selah!"*

Notes (anything I need to do/think differently/consider who needs to hear this, etc.):

Blessing 46: Faith on the Rise

Now is the time for a faith increase! You're ready to receive. Admittedly, you have already been given faith, for *"God has dealt to each one a measure of faith"* (Romans 12:3b). But God is always about abundance, about an increase, especially when it has to do with what He gives us, for the return must trump the investment.

So I bless you, _____, to not take your faith for granted but instead be a thankful recipient for what you've been bequeathed. And it is a given that your faith will be tested, for faith grows not in the gluttony of self but through the testing by fire, which results in the sacrifice of praise.

You're walking in tumultuous times. Faith is an action word; and, though it presents as a noun, it is a noun you must "have" to live victoriously, so I pray that you are blessed with a multiplied measure of faith. *"For we walk by faith, not by sight"* (2 Cor. 5:7). When Peter got out of the boat to walk, his faith was on the line. His faith stalled when he stopped walking and stopped looking at Jesus.

I bless you, _____, to surge ahead in your walk, not with blind attention but with a head start, because your gaze is locked on Jesus, for *"the head of every man is Christ"* (1 Cor. 11:3). Faith in Him will catapult you out of fear and into a future secure only in the One who has the end in sight.

Is your faith being stretched? Rejoice, for you are being called to a new level of intimacy with the Faith-Giver. And your faith walk is being culled and shaped so that you will bypass the detours and walk in step with Jesus.

When the mountain looms so large that it obstructs your view, you're being primed for persistence. In what area is your faith being tested? I bless you, _____, to push through the pain and the haze to discover who God is for you in this time of need.

It's all about Him. Do you truly see Him as your Comforter? Is He your Strong Tower? Can He possibly be your Provider, your Counselor, your Standby, the God who lifts your head? *"But without faith it is impossible to please Him, for he who comes to God must believe that He is, and that He is a rewarder of those who diligently seek Him"* (Hebrews 11:6). Oh, believe Him and seek Him!

I bless you, _____, to not falter on your faith walk. Your faith is on the rise, beloved child of God, and you will see Him if you keep walking, keep trusting, keep seeking, keep believing that He is the answer. *"For all the promises of God in Him are Yes, and in Him Amen, to the glory of God through us"* (2 Cor. 1:20).

I bless you, _____, to live out your faith in the juxtaposition of purpose and abandon, pushing through *"toward the goal for the prize of the upward call of God in Christ Jesus"* (Phil. 3:14), for He is *"the author and finisher of our faith"* (Hebrews 12:2).

Your faith, _____, is on the rise, for Jesus is ALIVE and His name is on the line. I bless you, forever and ever, in the name of Jesus, the name above all names!

Notes (anything I need to do/think differently/consider who needs to hear this, etc.):

Testimonial/feedback: "This blessing was read over me when I was deal-ing with difficulties and thinking that my closeness to God was being affected. This blessing encouraged me to see my faith as being stretched, not as my faith failing. I grew closer to God as a result."

BLESSING 47: GOD'S LULLABY

When you are on the verge of despair or disaster, Zephaniah 3:17 speaks into the darkness with the power and love of the Godhead. Listen to the words of this passage—a passage which has sometimes been referred to as God's lullaby: *"The LORD your God in your midst, the Mighty One, will save; He will rejoice over you with gladness, He will quiet you with His love, He will rejoice over you with singing."*

Labeled a lullaby because of the reassurance inherent in its message, these Spirit-inspired words leave no room for abandonment thinking. Two verses prior, a similar declaration of God's undeniable presence is penned: *"The King of Israel, the LORD,"* the second half of verse 15 proclaims, *"is in your midst. You shall see disaster no more."* Other biblical versions translate it as *"You shall **fear** disaster no more."* Fear and the Mighty One cannot coexist.

I bless you, _____, to grasp and cling to the visionary words of Zephaniah that are meant to shift your perspective. Even when disaster enters the scene of your life, fear is not to be the knee-jerk reaction, for your GOD is in the middle of it—for you!

He has not abandoned you nor forsaken you. He is not human in His responses to your cries for help. He is present. He is powerful. I bless you, _____, to not let fear intimidate you; instead, let the fear cower beneath the power of your GOD.

This lullaby has battle-cry intent. Oh, He is ready to save. This section of Scripture calls for God's people to rejoice, shout and sing in anticipation of God's faithfulness to deliver. _____, I bless you with celebratory praise that precedes your deliverance. You trust in the Lord who reminds you over and over not to fear because He is in the midst of the situation and lives in you.

The word trust, *"chesah"* in Hebrew, means *"to hope; to make someone a refuge."* That Someone is God. I bless you to rejoice and sing and exult in the Mighty One who is in your midst and in whom you trust. I bless your trust level to rise as you look to God as your refuge. And I bless you to joy in the Lord who *"has taken away your judgments; He has cast out your enemy"* (Zeph. 3:15).

Oh, for a thousand tongues to sing our great Redeemer's praise! God is all about redemption. He can release your pain. I bless you to let Him.

Have you ever heard such a beautiful refrain? This is the lullaby battle cry of a saving, singing, dancing, rejoicing, joy-filled God! I bless your ears to listen!

God rejoices over you with gladness!

God quiets you with His love.

He shushes you when you bring up past mistakes, for He has for-given you completely— to the uttermost—all of which you have repented.

God rejoices over you with singing!

Have your ears heard such a sound? I bless you, _____, to let God's songs reverberate through your heart so strongly that Papa's heartbeat eclipses yours.

Oh, how He loves you. Oh, how He delights in you. I bless you, _____, in the name of the MIGHTY ONE who always has the last word: *"I will deal with all who afflict you,"* says the Lord in verse 19 of the very same chapter in Zephaniah. *"I will save the lame and gather those who were driven out, I will appoint them for praise and fame in every land where they were put to shame."* You are appointed for praise! Trust Him!

Notes (anything I need to do/think differently/consider who needs to hear this, etc.):

BLESSING 48: NAMED

You have a name. Most likely it was given to you at birth by your parents. It's grown on you for better or for worse. You may prefer your middle over your first name, are halfhearted at best over your last name—or (less likely) quite pleased by them all.

God makes much ado about names. In the Old Testament, names declared something about a person, even if it had to do with their parents, as in the meaning of *"Isaac,"* translated as *"Laughter."* In both the Old and the New Testaments, God changed names. A name change spoke volumes about God's intention and view of an individual.

God's name is infinite in its splendor and authority. Listen to Jesus' prayer for His present and then future disciples in John 17: 11-12a: *"Now I am no longer in the world, but these are in the world, and I come to You. Holy Father, keep through Your name those whom You have given Me, that they may be one as We are. While I was with them in the world, I kept them in Your name."* I bless you, _____, to revel and take joy that you are kept in the name of the Father and the Son.

Being kept through the Father's name represents all that He is. Take note of the explicit emphasis on *"Holy"* Father. *"Holy"* is linked to *"set apart"* and *"sanctification."* God is so set apart from the world, so distinct and incredibly exalted in His attributes and actions that no one and nothing compares. No earthly being, no mythical genius can stand in the limelight of God and live.

Because you are kept in His name, you have been graced and granted the status of being completely clean and set apart for His use and His pleasure. I bless you, _____, to comprehend the spiritual authority and spiritual blessings you've been gifted through the Holy Father and His keeping you in His name.

You may have inherited a well-known name from your earthly father which has resulted in favor. But contrast that with *"Blessed be the God and Father of our Lord Jesus Christ, who has blessed us with every spiritual blessing in the heavenly places in Christ"* (Ephesians 1:3).

Your given name might be listed on an earthly roll call, but contrast that with the call to rejoice that your name is written in heaven (Luke 10:20).

Your name may even possibly open doors for opportunities, but nothing like John 14:13-14: *"And whatever you ask in My name, that I will do, that the Father may be glorified in the Son. If you ask anything in My name, I will do it."*

Don't miss, however, the purpose of receiving in the name of Jesus. It's for glory. Not yours, not mine, but for the glory of the Father and the Son. His name will forever be exalted—and your name will be transfigured by the Name above all Names.

I bless you, _____, to call upon His name often in praise and prayer. I bless you to rest in the keeping power of His name. And I bless you to speak of His name with the utmost awe that His name offers and engenders so that others will never doubt that He has named you as His own.

I bless you, _____, in the name of Jesus Christ of Nazareth, who spilled His blood so that you would be named in the scroll which He alone is worthy to open. And Jesus has declared to you the Father's name—as He says in the ending of His prayer in John 17:26— and will declare it, that the love with which the Father loves Him may be in you—and that He will be in you too (John 17:26). What a glorious name!

Notes (anything I need to do/think differently/consider who needs to hear this, etc.):

BLESSING 49: HIS LOVE NEVER FAILS

Failure. It's a word rife with meaning, overwhelmingly negative. We fear failure in all its forms. Whether we are the cause of it or the recipient of someone else's failure, we abhor it. We do what we can to evade it, hide it, push it as far from our consciousness as we can.

But God sees failure differently. For His children, God's redemptive touch transforms even the most debilitating failure. So I bless you, _____, with a God-heart response to failure.

Personal failure or the failure of others necessitates forgiveness. Forgiveness is the key to the transformation, as it unlocks the potential for a faith metamorphosis. When you fail, I bless you to receive forgiveness from the Giver of life. When others fail you, I bless you to forgive readily with the steadfast help of Christ, the Forgiver.

Personal failure can cause deep regret that leads to depression. When you fail as a result of sin, I bless you, _____, with the heart of David who penned in Psalm 51:10-11: *"Create in me a clean heart, O God, and renew a steadfast spirit within me. Do not cast me away from Your presence, and do not take Your Holy Spirit from me."* Repent and release it into the hands of God, who inspired John to write: *"If we confess our sins, He is faithful and just to forgive us our sins and to cleanse us from all unrighteousness"* (1 John 1:9). You are cleansed by the blood of Jesus.

In response to others' failures, I bless you with a Joseph heart that responded compassionately to his brothers who had sold him into slavery. *"Do not be afraid, for am I in the place of God?'"* Joseph said. *"But as for you, you meant evil against me; but God meant it for good, in order to bring it about as it is this day, to save many people alive. Now therefore, do not be afraid; I will provide for you and your little ones.' And he comforted them and spoke kindly to them"* (Genesis 50:19-21).

Failure is changed by forgiveness. And forgiveness is the love gift of God.

I bless you, _____, to have a radical mind reawakening, to have the mind of Christ. It's a shift in focus:

-It's not your life, but Christ in you.

-It's not your faith that falters, but His Spirit that can awaken you to new hope.

-It's not your forgiveness, but His that allows you to be free from the pain of failure— both yours and others.

-It's not your joy, but His that pours strength into you with a passion unmatched.

-It's not your presence, but Christ's that radiates peace unending.

-It's not your love, but His.

I bless you in the name of Jesus, whose love never fails, never loses hope, never wavers but always breathes and brings resurrection life to your mortal body so that LOVE rules and reigns in you. *"My flesh and my heart fail; but God is the strength of my heart and my portion forever"* (Psalm 73:26).

Receive His love.

Rest in His love.

Be refreshed in His love.

Be restored in His love.

Be renewed in His love.

Live in His love.

His love never fails.

His love never fails.

His love never fails.

Notes (anything I need to do/think differently/consider who needs to hear this, etc.):

Testimonial/feedback: "This blessing was such an encouragement! I've always been way too hard on myself if I don't meet either my own or the world's standards, and I've often considered myself a failure. God sees me differently than I see myself, and there's always redemption."

BLESSING 50: FILLED

_____, listen to the words of the Apostle Paul's prayer for those at Ephesus: *"For this reason I bow my knees to the Father of our Lord Jesus Christ, from whom the whole family in heaven and earth is named, that He would grant you, according to the riches of His glory, to be strengthened with might through His Spirit in the inner man, that Christ may dwell in your hearts through faith; that you, being rooted and grounded in love, may be able to comprehend with all the saints what is the width and length and depth and height— to know the love of Christ which passes knowledge; that you may be filled with all the fullness of God"* (Ephesians 3:14-19).

Did you catch the ending request? That you may be filled to all the fullness of God? The pathway to fullness is the love of Christ, so I bless you to let His love seep into every pore of your body, penetrate every cell and reverberate into every nook and cranny of your heart and mind. I bless you to receive Jesus' love in the fullest measure to stretch you beyond every limited perception.

This prayer by Paul is echoed throughout his letters in admonitions and encouragements:

"Let the word of Christ dwell in you richly in all wisdom..." (Colossians 3:16a).

"If we live in the Spirit, let us also walk in the Spirit" (Galatians 5:25).

"For it is God who works in you both to will and to do for His good pleasure" (Philippians 2:13).

"But we have this treasure in earthen vessels, that the excellence of the power may be of God and not of us" (2 Cor. 4:7).

So I bless you, _____, to be completely rooted and grounded in Christ's love. Water those love roots with constant attention and devotion to the Living Word. I bless you with pruning shears that cut off every counterfeit shoot so that you lavish your love on the One who died to bring you new life.

Be completely filled, _____. Make no provision for the flesh, but instead bask in the Spirit. I bless you to allow the fullness of God to tweak and turn the way you look at things. The fullness of God gives you a pertinent perspective for all that troubles you. The fullness of God overtakes self and pours glory into the mundane. The fullness of God generates gratefulness and tramples envy and discontent. The fullness of God overcomes half-heartedness and waywardness and protects your heart and mind.

So I bless you, _____, to be strengthened with might through His Spirit in the inner man. Be strengthened with all might, dearly beloved child of God, for you were called to display the fullness of God's power and love in all His glory!

I bless you in the name of Jesus of Nazareth, who empowers you to live a full life with the full extent of His love filling you and filling you and filling you to ALL fullness!

Notes (anything I need to do/think differently/consider who needs to hear this, etc.):

Blessing 51: Wise Waiting

Have you ever noticed how wisdom and waiting go hand in hand? That is—they do so if you want your wait to be inspired by and strengthened by God. And waiting is prime in God's kingdom, as illustrated in Isaiah 30:18: *"Therefore the Lord will wait, that He may be gracious to you; and therefore He will be exalted, that He may have mercy on you. For the Lord is a God of justice; blessed are all those who wait for Him."*

Is there something for which you are waiting? A healing, a reconciliation, a breakthrough, a promise yet fulfilled? In the Isaiah 30:18 passage, the Lord waits to be gracious to you. So there's much at stake in the waiting process. It's not for naught.

I bless you, _____, to wait wisely and perceive the Lord's waiting as grace to you. What if God was up to something more glorious in your wait than you could conceive?

Don't miss the wording at the end of the passage: *"Blessed are those who wait for Him."* Not blessed are those who wait for the fulfillment of their wait. That kind of waiting generally results in frustration and anxiety. Here's where God's wisdom in the wait appears.

Listen to it again: *"Blessed are those who wait for Him."* The focus is intentional. God is the Author and Finisher of your faith, and you are not waiting for something but Someone—the One who will bring it to pass.

So I bless you, _____, to wait for God, with a passion that relegates angst out of the picture. Your God will come through. Look to Him! Learn from Him! When the wait seems interminably long, ask Him for more wisdom in the wait, and He will give it to you generously and without reproach (James 1:5). His wisdom will be first of all *"pure, then peaceable, gentle, willing to yield, full of mercy and good fruits, without partiality and without hypocrisy"* (James 3:17).

I bless you, _____, with a view off the wait and onto the God who waits to be gracious to you. I bless you to be open to hear from the Giver of every good gift who will be willing to share if the gift you want differs from what He intends to give. And I bless you to believe His Word and trust His ways and to find contentment in Him as you wait.

I bless you with a faith increase, a God-exalting reservoir of praise and a heart of thankfulness, all of which will keep you steady in the wait.

I bless you, _____, in the name of the Lord who waits for you and who calls you blessed for waiting for Him.

Notes (anything I need to do/think differently/consider who needs to hear this, etc.):

BLESSING 52: ALL COVERED

_____, listen to the words inscribed in Scripture to bless you: *"And God is able to make all grace abound toward you, that you, always having all sufficiency in all things, may have an abundance for every good work"* (2 Corinthians 9:8).

The word *"all"* is repeated thrice in this one passage; four times if you count the prefix *"al"* in *"always."* Such repetition in Scripture is intentional in its inclusion. Don't miss God's heart for you in this verse. Even if it's been a *"nothing"* sort of season for you—where nothing has seemingly gone right—God's Word stands in stark contrast to the enemy's clamoring that you've been left uncovered by God.

Be blessed, then, _____, with God's whole heart for you. Where He's concerned, He has *"all"* in mind for you. In context, this verse refers to material means, but God's Word often has multiple meanings to speak into a myriad of situations, many intensely personal and certainly purposeful.

_____, God is able to make ALL grace abound toward you, so that you, ALL-ways having ALL sufficiency in ALL things, may have an abundance for every good work. There's no *"less-than"* wording in this passage.

Be encouraged, dearly beloved child of God—that God is ALL about what He's doing in your life. I bless you to partake of His profuse grace that affords you with His sufficiency so that you will never be deficient. I bless you with seeing Him work in provisionary measures that astound you with His creativity, and I bless you to watch His grace impact every sphere of your life.

Rest assured, _____, that God will indeed multiply every seed that you have sown. He has taken exclusive notice of your cheerful giving of all that concerns you, and He eagerly awaits your expression of gratitude when He brings forth the fruit of your labors.

_____, blessed are you who fears the Lord. You embrace and relish His commandments, and so your children will be mighty on the earth. You are blessed because of the stand you take. Your house will not lack wealth for you are generous with all your gifts. Sunrise will break through the darkness, for God is gracious and full of compassion, and He is righteous. Because you lend willingly and with grace, God will direct your steps with His generous wisdom. You will not be shaken, and your exemplary reputation will be lasting *(based on Psalm 112:1-6).*

I bless you, _____, with a ready heart, trusting in God, your spirit unperturbed and open to the ministering work of the Spirit as you place ALL things into His hands for Him to work exceedingly abundantly above all that you ask or think.

I bless you in the name of God the Father and His Son Jesus, who have curtailed the enemy's control for now and will obliterate it for eternity. According to 1 Cor. 15:28: *"Now when all things are made subject to Him, then the Son Himself will also be subject to Him who put all things under Him, that God may be all in all."*

God is your all in all, dearest _____. He is your everything, and He has your ALL in His loving control.

Notes (anything I need to do/think differently/consider who needs to hear this, etc.):

Testimonial/feedback: *""Wow! Ruth called (and I hear from her at most a few times a year) and told me that she felt led to call and read me this specific blessing. Very timely and very appropriate! I needed to hear it. Her call could not have come at a better time. We ended up praying, and this blessing was the stimulus to me forgiving someone. God does have my 'all' covered."*

BLESSING 53: JOY CHOICE

_____, I bless you with ears attentive to the Word of God, just as the people in Ezra's day responded to the reading of God's Word recorded in Nehemiah 8. *"And Ezra opened the book in the sight of all the people, for he was standing above all the people; and when he opened it, all the people stood up. And Ezra blessed the LORD, the great God. Then all the people answered, 'Amen, Amen!' while lifting up their hands. And they bowed their heads and worshiped the LORD with their faces to the ground"* (Nehemiah 8:5-6).

The Word of God elicits response in the believer. I bless you to be alert to the still, small voice of God; to His voice that thunders like lightening; and to His commands of blessing sown throughout Scripture. His Word is never to be commandeered without a Spirit response that breathes life and meaning into your life.

God knows exactly what He wants to get through to you. In Nehemiah 8, the Levites helped the people understand the reading. You, _____, have been blessed with the Spirit, described in part as your Counselor and Teacher. He will lead you into all truth.

"And Nehemiah, who was the governor, Ezra the priest and scribe, and the Levites who taught the people said to all the people, 'This day is holy to the LORD your God; do not mourn nor weep.' For all the people wept,

when they heard the words of the Law" (Nehemiah 8:9). The people in Nehemiah's day were given instruction in how to respond. They wept, and God has times where weeping is absolutely appropriate, but not for them this day. In verse 10, Ezra says, "*Go your way, eat the fat, drink the sweet, and send portions to those for whom nothing is prepared; for this day is holy to our Lord. Do not sorrow, for the joy of the LORD is your strength.*'"

I bless you, _____, to draw from this passage the heart intent of God. Today may be your day to rejoice. Think of the practical instruction in James 1:2-4 to "*Count it all joy when you fall into various trials, knowing that the testing of your faith produces patience. But let patience have its perfect work, that you may be perfect and complete, lacking nothing.*" Are you in the midst of a trial? Wouldn't it make more sense to count it all worthwhile? After all, a trial meant to make you complete through patience could easily be considered worthwhile.

But joy? Think about it. If God says to count a trial in terms of joy, then He has an attitude adjustment in mind. _____, I bless you to *joy* today if you are beset with a trial. I bless you to draw on the joy of the Lord if you are in need of strength. And I bless you with a joy attitude adjustment that will depress the enemy.

Joy is your birthright as a child of the King, "*for the kingdom of God is not eating and drinking, but righteousness and peace and joy in the Holy Spirit*" (Romans 14:17). The angels experience joy when one sinner repents (Luke 15:10). Joy is linked to peace in believing so that God will make you abound in hope by the power of the Holy Spirit (Romans 15:13). Your joy may be full when you ask and receive in Jesus' name (John 16:24). And no one can take away your joy from you when you see Jesus again (John 16:22).

The Apostle Paul made prayer requests with all joy and said that his joy would be fulfilled when the Philippians would be like-minded and unified in love (Phil. 1:4; 2:2). Joy is a vital and victorious part of the kingdom of God.

So I bless you, _____, and speak over you the precious and powerful Word of God as inscribed in Scripture in Psalm 16:11: *"You will show me the path of life; in Your presence is fullness of joy; at Your right hand are pleasures forevermore."* Be blessed today with the fullness of joy in the presence of the Lord!

Notes (anything I need to do/think differently/consider who needs to hear this, etc.):

Testimonial/feedback: "When going through various trials, it has been my privilege to have my precious friend Ruth by my side equipped with powerful prayers and blessings. I would be hard pressed to say which one is my favorite, but it's probably the one that ministers to me right when I'm going through difficult circumstances."

BLESSING 54: THE CHALLENGE

_____, what if you took God's challenge to allow one seven-word biblical passage to change your day? If you knew that taking God at His Word in Philippians 2:14 would make you His light-bearer and would silence the enemy as you surrender your mind and words in obedience, would you take Him up on it?

I bless you, _____, to relish the challenge that God presents. I bless you to tackle it wholeheartedly. And I bless you to reap the real rewards offered by the One who has your best at heart.

What are the seven words? Listen intently. Listen with expectancy. Listen with the Spirit in you opening your ears to receive this dynamic dare issued by God through the Apostle Paul to the church at Philippi. _____, *"do all things without complaining and disputing."* Listen again. _____, do all things without complaining and disputing.

The Amplified Bible adds a little deeper understanding that unearths motives. *"Do all things,"* the Amplified translation begins, *"without grumbling and faultfinding and complaining (against God) and questioning and doubting (among yourselves)."*

Suddenly, what we could try to shift onto a bad day, a bad mood or unwelcome circumstances becomes an affront against God. Have you ever connected those dots? Have you ever considered that your complaining meant that you were unhappy with God? I bless your understanding of this passage, _____, to pierce your heart.

We readily believe that the complaining of the Israelites in the desert was against God; after all, they received manna from heaven and complained. They saw the miraculous and grumbled. Their wilderness wandering didn't dent their shoes or cause sores on their feet. But that didn't lead them to praise; instead, their focus generated pouting. God had victory in mind for them. The desert would lead to the land overflowing with milk and honey and promise and potential, but they forfeited the blessing.

Did you ever wonder if there were some in their midst who were thankful and awestruck by God's goodness and glory but allowed the doubts and questions of others to catapult them to criticism and complaint?

Oh, I bless you, _____, to live your days and nights with the glory of God foremost on your mind and inscribed on your heart. I bless you to take every thought captive to Jesus Christ so that your freedom is secure. I bless your thought life and your emotions to display Jesus magnified and circumstances diminished.

Your thoughts and feelings do dictate how you *"do"* life. So I bless you to have the mind of Christ so that everything you do is devoid of anger against God. Instead, I bless you, _____, to be content in all things.

And, _____, I bless you to be the thought-changer among your friends and family who are struggling and in despair. I bless your questions to center on how God can be seen in you and who He is for you right now. Don't question God to others but ask Him how He is to be exalted in your comings and your goings and your doings. Love Him. Rest in Him. Talk to Him. Enjoy Him. Praise Him. Do all for Him.

You are blessed. Don't forget it. And, _____, hear the promise written and God-breathed to you as you choose to engage this challenge: *"Do all things without complaining or disputing, that you may become blameless and harmless, children of God without fault in the midst of a crooked and perverse generation, among whom you shine as lights in the world"* (Phil. 2:14-15).

Oh, I bless you, _____, to shine brilliantly in your generation, reflecting the radiance of God who challenges you to think and live boldly and brightly. Shine with His glory so that all will see how much He loves you and how much you honor Him, believe Him, love Him and obey Him!

Notes (anything I need to do/think differently/consider who needs to hear this, etc.):

BLESSING 55: INSCRIBED FOR ETERNITY

_____, it's time to remember some things that you may have forgotten. Listen to the word of the Lord as penned by the prophet Isaiah for your profit: *"See, I have inscribed you on the palms of My hands; your walls are continually before Me"* (Isaiah 49:16).

In context, this passage is speaking of God's forever affection for His chosen people. Those in Zion at the time of Isaiah thought that God had forgotten them. God's response is clear: *"Can a woman forget her nursing child, and not have compassion on the son of her womb? Surely they may forget; yet I will not forget you"* (Isaiah 49:15).

You, _____, are God's chosen child. He will not and cannot forget you. Though you may feel at times that He has, that is not the truth. His care for you exceeds human understanding.

God uses His hands as a metaphor over and over for power and victory and honor and blessing. Listen to a few scriptural examples.

Exodus 15:16 recounts victory attributed to God's hand: *"Your right hand, O Lord, has become glorious in power; Your right hand, O Lord, has dashed the enemy in pieces."*

I bless you, _____, to place every troubling situation into God's hand and trust that He will defeat the enemy as you look to Him, giving God free reign with the timing and the means and the outcome. I bless you to use your hands in the authority of Jesus to silence the enemy and watch God gloriously bring deliverance.

The saving power of God's hand is reiterated in Psalm 138:7: *"Though I walk in the midst of trouble, You will revive me; You will stretch out Your hand against the wrath of my enemies, and Your right hand will save me."* I bless you, _____, with the revival mindset of the Most High, who delivers you with purposeful intent. I bless you to draw from His well of wisdom all the days of your life.

Mark 16:19 underscores the honor attributed to God's hand: *"So then, after the Lord had spoken to them, He was received up into heaven, and sat down at the right hand of God."* I bless you, _____, with awe-inspiring views of God that elicit praise for the One who has captured your heart and your soul. And I bless you to touch others with your hands stretched out with His emblazoned with your name and experience His saving power magnified to bring Him great glory.

And lastly, John 10:27-29 portrays the keeping power of God's hand: *"My sheep hear My voice, and I know them, and they follow Me. And I give them eternal life, and they shall never perish; neither shall anyone snatch them out of My hand. My Father, who has given them to Me, is greater than all; and no one is able to snatch them out of My Father's hand."*

I bless you, _____, with undeterred confidence in the Father, who was and is and shall be victorious in your life, here and forever. I bless you to align your heart, mind, and soul with the Holy Spirit, who is sealed and seared upon your spirit. And I bless you in the name of Jesus of Nazareth, who traversed the Calvary road with the cross on His back and your name inscribed on His palms. When the nail pierced His hands, His blood poured forth over every one of your sins and brought victory and power and honor and blessing to you.

And the words of Isaiah, *"See, I have inscribed you on the palms of My hands"* written hundreds of years before— reached a prophetic culmination no one but God could foresee. Jesus revealed the wounds on His hands to irrefutably prove He was risen indeed. Your name, _____, inscribed on His palms, and His scars—will remain forever as a testament to God's victory and power and honor and blessing.

I bless you, _____ _____, to grasp God's handhold with eyes of wonder and eyes enlightened to know the hope of His calling, His rich, glorious inheritance in the saints, and His exceedingly great power to you, for you believe (Ephesians 1:18-19)!

Notes (anything I need to do/think differently/consider who needs to hear this, etc.):

Blessing 56: Night Song

Oh, _____, you've known troubles and trials. It's a given, for life on earth falls far short of heaven's glory. James pens the words of *"Consider it all joy* **when** *you encounter various trials"* in chapter one of his Holy-Spirit inspired book, cluing us into the commonality of trials, as well as their potential for the believer.

I bless you, _____, as you face your current trial. I bless you with God's heart for you and the beauty of His presence in you and your difficulties.

Psalm 42 explicitly reveals the candid cry of one overcome by trouble but whose voice resonates with hope borne out of intimacy with God. Listen, _____, to the well-known words of verse one: *"As the deer pants for the water brooks, so pants my soul for You, O God."*

In 1981 Marth Nystrom wrote a familiar praise and worship song, *As the Deer*, based on this verse. It's a beautiful melody with striking words. But it doesn't begin to capture the desperation of the psalmist who was clamoring for help and drowning in dire circumstances.

In fact, verse seven of Psalm 42: *"Deep calls unto deep at the noise of Your waterfalls; all Your waves and billows have gone over me"* is a vivid description of the psalmist's overwhelming trials. And yet it's also a prayer song of one desperate for the intimate touch from the God he knows on a deep level. _____, that is your heart cry.

The God who knows you and your comings and goings—and every word on your tongue before it is spoken; the God who formed you marvelously in your mother's womb; the God who calls you by name and has called you from darkness to light—will see you through this hardship.

I bless you with jubilant hope in Him. I bless you with a deep, abiding, constant call of eager longing to draw ever nearer to Him. I encourage you to yearn for His touch and to experience it in a way that ministers intimately so that His love and His Spirit pour over you with greater intensity than the trouble that threatens to drown your hope and lay claim to your faith.

Verse eight of Psalm 42 speaks—no, sings—of this blessed hope: *"The Lord will command His lovingkindness in the daytime, and in the night His song shall be with me—a prayer to the God of my life."* And this verse is a beacon of blessing positioned intentionally between the psalmist's questioning and his cries for assistance. It stands as a testimony to God's character and His ever-present help.

_____, listen again to the life-inspiring words: *"The Lord will command His lovingkindness in the daytime, and in the night His song shall be with me—a prayer to the God of my life."* Let those words ring through your mind and your spirit.

_____, I pray for your days to reveal God's love in a myriad of ways that will both take your breath away and breathe expectation and endurance into your very being. This is warrior talk of emotional and experiential significance.

Our reigning, victorious Lord will command His lovingkindness in the daytime for you, _____. Don't ever doubt it. Look for

His timing and His ways in the most insignificant and yet compelling details, for He is a master at weaving His love through means that bespeak His glory and His goodness.

And I encourage you, _____, with God's promise that His song shall be with you—a prayer to the God of your life. I bless you with His refrain holding you steady when night descends. I bless your night seasons to be rich and full and replete with the sweetness of God's tenderness. And I bless you with words He gives you to sing back to Him so that you harmonize with God's heart for you.

It will be a song like no other, and you will sing with abandon to and with the One who descends into the depths with you. And when the waves threaten to crash, He will transform the sound to a hymn of faith that echoes into the spiritual realm with reverberating praise.

I urge you, _____, to sing, and I bless you in the name of God Almighty, your strength and shield. He alone is your heart's desire, and only He can satisfy. Never cease to sing God's night song, for He will serenade you with it.

Notes (anything I need to do/think differently/consider who needs to hear this, etc.):

Testimonial/feedback: "I feel confident in reading a blessing to someone else, because there is so much truth in it from God's Word. I know that I am representing what He says and have seen people get touched by the truth."

BLESSING 57: WORRY NOT

_____, your life is in the hands of God, who delights to care for you. He is your Shepherd, your Provider, your Deliverer, your Help, the Mighty God who makes a way for you and the Giver of every good and perfect gift. He is with you. He is present. He is powerful. He stands when you can't. He watches over you through the night. He is the great I AM, and every word He speaks comes to pass.

See God for who He is. I bless you, _____, to worry not for all worry is naught. It's worthless. More than that, it's troublesome. It steals your time and robs you of your joy. I bless you to make an intentional choice to catch yourself when you worry and throw your worries at the Lord.

After all, He commands us in Philippians 4 to _"be anxious for nothing."_ Instead, we are to come to Him with our anxieties and worries. So I bless you, _____, to treat your worries like a hot potato and throw them to Him before you get burned.

Just don't forget the caveat. You hand over your worries with thanksgiving. Listen to all the words of verse 6 in Philippians 4: _"Be anxious for nothing, but in everything by prayer and supplication, with thanksgiving, let your requests be made known to God."_ Oh, yes, beloved, God didn't haphazardly include thanksgiving. God is onto something transforming here. Worry and thanksgiving just don't mix. They literally cannot coexist.

Words of thankfulness will change your heart as you pour out your troubles to the One who hears with both ear and heart. I bless you, _____, to render worry worthless as you tally up all the ways you are thankful to God. I bless you to steep yourself in gratitude and slough off anxiety. Take God literally at His Word! Make a conscious choice to trade your heavy heart as you look at God's heart for you.

Has He not promised to carry your burdens? YES!

Hasn't He said that He knows your weaknesses and that He will be your strength in the midst of them all? YES!

Will He not complete what He has started in you? YES!

Can He ever forget you? NO!

_____, I bless you and challenge you to do what God commands in Philippians 4:6.

Worry is not an emotion that God endorses.

You know which emotions are God-endorsed, and they are the byproduct of a Spirit-controlled life. So I bless you to check your worries in with the One who wants full control of you—body, mind and soul—and surrender them in exchange for His joy and His peace.

It's an exchange that leads to abundant life, and you'll never regret it. I bless you in the name of Jesus, the Prince of Peace, who lives in you and desires to have full reign and authority so that His banner of love over you will ward off all worry.

Notes (anything I need to do/think differently/consider who needs to hear this, etc.):

Blessing 58: Give Up

Sometimes the struggle seems too strong, too potent of a pull to resist. But you, _____, were called for yes, such a time as this. A time that threatens to tax your resources. A time that demands more than you have. A time that brings you to your knees.

I bless you, _____, to bow not in terror at the trouble but bow before your God, who responds to cries of weakness with unquenchable warrior power.

Giving up—in God's terminology—is the beginning of your answer. In earthly terms, it is seen as a negative reaction, but not in God's dictionary. In God-speak, giving up is preferable, a prerequisite to victory. For God's children, giving up means releasing all that binds you to distress.

I bless you, _____, to give up in ALL insurmountable situations.

What might that look like?

I bless you to release your expectations of the solution.

I bless you to relinquish the outcome to God.

I bless you to not tamper with the process.

I bless you to renege on your propensity to panic.

And I bless you to limit your control to your attitude and your view of God.

You can't do the impossible. Even the improbable is beyond your ability. But God often turns the tables on your trials when you exchange places with Him. I bless you to give up and let Him be in charge.

I bless you, _____, in the name of the omnipotent God, who is the lifter of your head and the lover of your soul, the God who never gives up on you and who is wholeheartedly for you even when you can't see Him at work.

He is the invisible, unimaginably creative, incomprehensibly compassionate, and incredibly intentional God who will guide you through this time in His inimitable way. Give up and let Him lead for *"the Lord, He is the One who goes before you. He will be with you, He will not leave you nor forsake you; do not fear nor be dismayed"* (Deuteronomy 31:8).

Notes (anything I need to do/think differently/consider who needs to hear this, etc.):

Testimonial/feedback: "God has ministered to me through these biblical blessings, and I've found God never wastes our trials. Instead, He enables us to come alongside others who are going through various trials. It's been my privilege to share some of the blessings with friends and co-workers. One friend needed wisdom in raising her children, and she was able to share blessings with her son that helped him see the high calling God has on his life. Another friend was feeling overwhelmed by the weight of responsibilities and was reminded that God is walking with her though these trials—that God never meant for her to carry them alone."

BLESSING 59: FAITH FOR THE LONG HAUL

Let's face it: we like to see good things happen quickly. In our society, quick fixes are expected. But God knows best, and many results that He has in mind are not only worth waiting for, they literally can't be accomplished in a short span of time.

_____, I bless you to be open to God's timetable to accomplish His best for you and in you.

Take character, for example. How many people do you know who became patient overnight? How many prideful people exhibit humility within a week's time? Or morose individuals consistently joyful after a month?

God can and does do miracles in people's lives that change their demeanor and outlook; however, more than likely, those "quick change" miracles were oftentimes long in the making. Addictions have been broken—seemingly overnight—by God's grace, but more than likely you can account that miracle to long seasons of prayer.

I encourage you, _____, to persevere in prayer for such miracles for you and your loved ones. I bless you with as much expectancy after months of prayer as when you first begun. And I bless you to urge others to stay the course when their faith falters.

Biblical faith that stands on the promises of God is always forged over the long haul. The passage of Scripture that is defined as a hymn of faith in the book of Habakkuk illustrates this. Listen to the words penned by the prophet Habakkuk when facing potential disaster: *"Though the fig tree may not blossom, nor fruit be on the vines; though the labor of the olive may fail, and the fields yield no food; though the flock may be cut off from the fold, and there be no herd in the stalls —Yet I will rejoice in the Lord, I will joy in the God of my salvation"* (Habakkuk 3:17-18).

This is not flippant faith that sizzles and soon disappears. The tension of what *"may be"* hangs in the balance, but it does not deter the prophet from proclaiming his confidence in God. _____, I entreat you to rest in God no matter His timing or His choice of outcome. I bless you to trust in God when the going is tougher than you could have imagined.

And I urge you to stand firm when the future seems dim, confident that God can intervene and will if that is what would benefit you most.

Some people tie faith to trusting God when you *"know"* the outcome will be horrific, as in "I *know* things will never change (or calamity *will* come), but I trust God regardless." Habakkuk doesn't do that. He proclaims faith as trust when the tension is the strongest, not the answer the dimmest.

The fig tree may not blossom, but it also may. Faith is trusting God knows best and comforts best and guides best and cares best. So I exhort you not to immediately proclaim the worst, but to trust in God's unrivaled best.

I bless you, _____, in the name of Almighty God, El Shaddai. His Holy Spirit inspired Habakkuk to write the perfect ending to the hymn of faith: *"The Lord God is my Strength, my personal bravery, and my invincible army; He makes my feet like hinds' feet and will make me to walk [not to stand still in terror, but to walk] and make [spiritual] progress upon my high places [of trouble, suffering, or responsibility]"* (Habakkuk 3:19, Amplified Bible).

I bless you to rejoice in your God who—as the Author and Finisher of your faith—will see you through to His victory, which is your victory as well—in His unparalleled time and way.

Notes (anything I need to do/think differently/consider who needs to hear this, etc.):

Testimonial/feedback: "I felt led to bring this blessing to church one morning. I ended up reading it over one of the nursery workers, and she started sobbing and asked for a copy."

BLESSING 60: MERCY RESPONSE

Have you ever felt that you have been judged unjustly? Maybe it was something you said that caused someone to look at you with different eyes. Perhaps you have felt that your motives were in question. Or maybe you've felt that others have questioned your work abilities, your spiritual progress or even the way you do things or how you look.

Or maybe it's less about you and more about your loved ones or friends who have come under the scrutiny of others. Whatever the situation, _____, it's more than likely you have experienced the judgment of others that has caused you some angst.

_____, the Word of God frees you from the judgment of others and the propensity to judge in response. *"Judge not, and you shall not be judged"* from Luke 6:37a is such a well-known passage that most can recite it with ease. However, it's much more difficult to take to heart—both in action and response. After all, if we—or those we love—are being judged, an automatic response is to feel hurt and thereby judge in return.

I bless you, _____, to understand the freedom that comes from following God's command to judge not.

Oh, it's doable. Not in your own strength, of course. But God isn't laying the impossible in your lap. In fact, He's not laying it in your lap at all. He's asking you to hand it to Him. HE is the Judge. And He has generously given you a gift of grace and compassion as you give Him the condemnation, the shame, the looks, the words, the disdain and the hopelessness.

If you are—or have been—under any of these, I bless you to hand the condemnation and the condemners over to God. I bless you to not allow the poison of judgment to infiltrate your heart so that you find yourself in the same position as those who have judged you. And I bless you to respond with reconciliation in mind, even if it seems futile.

_____, pray that those who have judged you or others you love will experience the same mercy and grace and peace that you so desperately need when you have failed. I bless you with the mercy response of the Most High, who encourages you to *"love your enemies, bless those who curse you, do good to those who hate you, and pray for those who spitefully use you and persecute you, that you may be sons of your Father in heaven; for He makes His sun rise on the evil and on the good, and sends rain on the just and on the unjust"* (Matthew 5:44-45).

I bless you, _____, in the name of Jehovah God, who judges justly and who judges by the blood of Jesus. And the blood of Jesus washes you clean from every conviction of the Spirit that you have confessed—and brings forgiveness, newness, life and healing. That life, in turn, sets you free from judging others as well.

_____, live under the glorious covering of the blood of Jesus and be a mercy-bearer and grace-giver!

Notes (anything I need to do/think differently/consider who needs to hear this, etc.):

BLESSING 61: ABUNDANCE BEHIND AND AHEAD

_____, the year prior and the year ahead have been earmarked for abundance. You might initially disagree with that assessment of your past year, but *"abundance"* in God's lexicon is sometimes defined differently than Webster's Dictionary. So, still your mind so you can put this in perspective with Psalm 65 as your backdrop.

Listen to the words magnificently recorded by David under inspiration of the Holy Spirit: *"Blessed is the man You choose, and cause to approach You, that he may dwell in Your courts. We shall be satisfied with the goodness of Your house, of Your holy temple"* (Psalm 65:4).

_____, you have been chosen by God to draw near to Him and find indulgence in intimacy with Him. You have been sealed for satisfaction that grasps the goodness of the Most High. I bless you to rejoice in His choice of you for far more than what most long for in this life.

I bless you to tarry long in His presence. And I bless you to joy in His abundant provision of Himself for you and your family so that you never sense lack when it comes to anything that pertains to your physical, emotional and spiritual needs.

Verse 11 of Psalm 65 is the verse that defines your destiny. Listen to the Spirit speak through David as he writes of his God: *"You crown the year with Your goodness, and Your paths drip with abundance."* The year that David spoke of thousands of years ago is this year for you. Webster's defines abundance as: *"1). an ample quantity: profusion; and 2). affluence, wealth."*

Don't be too quick to discount this definition for you. While Webster and most who read his commentary would couch these adjectives in earthly terms, you stand under the profuse outpouring of God's blessings and His Spirit's power—and His spiritual terminology is vastly more descriptive and prescriptive for your life. I bless you, _____, to take explicit note of God's goodness.

Even in trials and troubles, God reigns. You have traversed His path laid out specifically for you. Not all earthly paths drip with abundance, but His does. I bless you with thankfulness for His calling and your response to His call. When His call breeds difficulty, I bless you to see Him with greater clarity—God on the throne and His ear ever closer to your calls and cries of need, of petition, of praise.

Listen to verses 5-8 of this psalm: *"By awesome deeds in righteousness You will answer us, O God of our salvation. You who are the confidence of all the ends of the earth, and of the far-off seas; who established the mountains by His strength, being clothed with power. You who still the noise of the seas, the noise of their waves, and the tumult of the peoples. They also who dwell in the farthest parts are afraid of Your signs; You make the outgoings of the morning and evening rejoice."*

_____, you know His power. You speak—and comprehend by experience—that He is your confidence, and you have seen Him at work. I bless you to disciple others in the goodness of God. I bless you to be a living exhibition of His power. And I bless you to point people toward—and participate in—the praise that brings the greatest glory to God. For He has called you to dwell in His courts and to call His people to join you in celebrating His goodness and His power.

Listen once more to Psalm 65:11 for you. _____, God crowns your years with His goodness, and His paths drip with abundance. He is generous with you and for you.

And now be attentive to the ending of this psalm: *"They drop on the pastures of the wilderness, and the little hills rejoice on every side. The pastures are clothed with flocks; the valleys also are covered with grain; They shout for joy, they also sing."* God's abundance drops on the wilderness. So your times of greatest trial will experience a downpour of God's intervention and your years of drought will be reviewed in light of God's intentional goodness.

Oh, if you could only see what God has been up to for you. But then you would be walking by sight. God has far more ahead for you than you could ever conceive. I bless you, _____, to forge ahead in faith that your years are blessed by God.

So, go ahead and shout. Move forward with singing. Enter His gates with thanksgiving and His courts with praise. Abundance is your birthright—and will define your future. You are blessed with God's abundance and your years are crowned with His goodness. Rejoice!

Notes (anything I need to do/think differently/consider who needs to hear this, etc.):

Blessing 62: Persistence

God is all about persistence. Have you ever thought about that? He never gives up or leaves a task unfinished—and that applies specifically to you and the situations that concern you. He sees things through and wants you to join Him in the pursuit of completion. Will you take Him up on this bold venture? It will cost you sweat, tears, and time, but you will experience those same things anyway whether or not you choose to persist with God. The persistence route leads to glory in the midst of the trial; the other leads through much condemnation and despair.

So I bless you, ____ _____, to join God in fellowship as you embark upon this journey, a journey that will result in a greater, multi-faceted completion than you could ever envision at the starting line, *"for it is God who works in you both to will and to do for His good pleasure"* (Philippians 2:13).

Godly persistence, is well…persistence. It's not simple agreement with the One who created you and calls you by name. It's not a haphazard wayward trek through uncharted territory without direction. It's gritty, it's determined, it reeks of downright radical reorganizing and it has compelling potential.

Therefore, I bless you, _____, with God-given stamina from the very start. And if you chose not to sign up for the persistence path in your current trial, you're most likely still at the starting point, so I encourage you to stand up and move with renewed vigor and upturned face toward the Victor.

To persist is the opposite of resist. You resist the enemy, but you persist with God. And God never asks us to persist alone but instead calls us to gain ground with Him. _____, I bless you with the fullness of His presence, fully aware of the nuances of His nearness and His still, small voice that resonates through the storm. I bless you to call upon Him for wisdom and to write it down on the recesses of your heart—at the ready for whenever you need it.

And when He calls you to rest from the battle so that He can take the lead, I bless you to let Him. Don't ever pick up your weapon of choice and go it alone. You have the offensive weapons of the Word and prayer, which are saturated with Spirit power and God's presence.

I bless you, _____, in the name of the Lord, for He *"is my strength and song, and He has become my salvation; He is my God, and I will praise Him; my father's God, and I will exalt Him. The Lord is a man of war; the Lord is His name"* (Exodus 15:2-3).

I bless you to persist, abide, endure, pursue, prevail, persevere and linger long with the One who will see you through triumphantly to where you can proclaim with the Apostle Paul in 2 Timothy 4:7: *"I have fought the good fight, I have finished the race, I have kept the faith."*

Notes (anything I need to do/think differently/consider who needs to hear this, etc.):

BLESSING 63: DEFIANT JOY

Joy is your calling as a child of God. But it generally doesn't come upon you as does happiness when you have something wonderful happen to you. It's not a happenstance calling but a pursuit of deliberate intention. I bless you, _____, to lay hold of the Lord's joy with purposeful resolve.

Such resolve smacks of strength; and, indeed, joy and strength are linked in Scripture with repentance, as in Nehemiah 8:10b: *"Do not sorrow, for the joy of the Lord is your strength."* Did you notice that it's not your joy but the Lord's? And the package deal of joy and strength is far better than one without the other? _____, I bless you to allow the joy of the Lord to overcome all sorrow that your sin or others' sin has caused you.

Allow Him to bring it to mind, so that you can confess and/or forgive with His help. Call to Him, and He will answer you. Forgive those who have contributed to the demise of joy and peace in your life.

And ask God to illuminate any area in your life or heart that has kept you from experiencing His joy.

Any unbelief? *"Now may the God of hope fill you with all joy and peace in believing, that you may abound in hope by the power of the Holy Spirit"* (Romans 15:13).

Any pride standing in the way? *"The humble also shall increase their joy in the Lord"* (Isaiah 29:19a).

A reduction in rejoicing in the Lord and praising Him? *"Oh come, let us sing to the Lord! Let us shout joyfully to the Rock of our salvation"* (Psalm 95:1).

I bless you with allowing the Lord's joy to penetrate and saturate and move in and through all circumstances in your life that would cause you to doubt God's goodness, purpose and heart for you. I bless you with such a joy penetration that His strength will rise in you and you will declare His goodness over you and all that concerns you.

I bless you with defiant joy that stands on God's Word and His promises and His love for you and defies the enemy's attempt to destroy your confidence in who God is and who you are in His sight.

I bless you, _____, in the name of Jesus, the Joy-Giver and the Joy-Bearer, who loves you with His unending love and in whom you will declare with the prophet Habakkuk: *"Yet I will rejoice in the Lord, I will joy in the God of my salvation"* (Habakkuk 3:18).

Notes (anything I need to do/think differently/consider who needs to hear this, etc.):

Testimonial/feedback: "What a blessing this book will be to so many! How refreshing and life giving it has been to have these words of truth read over me!"

Blessing 64: Convenience at Stake

Convenience is not a biblical word. It stifles the Spirit like many other cultural words of our day. Convenience smells of self; and when the Spirit and self collide, convenience has to go. So I bless you, _____ _____, to evaluate convenience's place on your priority list.

Convenience is overtly exclusive in regards to self. It includes preference and often excludes impartiality. It includes gratification and usually excludes sacrifice.

God, on the other hand, is overtly all-inclusive when it comes to developing your character. He flat-out doesn't give us a choice in regards to thanksgiving, for He says in 1 Thessalonians 5:18: *"In everything give thanks; for this is the will of God in Christ Jesus for you."* We can't be thankful only when it's convenient for us.

Or consider Philippians 4:6: *"Be anxious for nothing, but in everything by prayer and supplication, with thanksgiving, let your requests be made known to God."* (There's that thanksgiving word again.) And He also includes the "everything" word again. He wants you to run everything that brings anxiety by Him, so you don't cut Him out of His counseling and comforting role. So, _____, I bless you with an anti-convenience view of talking to God.

"Trust in the Lord with all your heart, and lean not on your own under-standing. In all your ways acknowledge Him, and He shall direct your paths" (Proverbs 3:5-6). I bless you, _____, to link every critical decision with a dependence upon God.

Trust and obey are God's coupled convenience-blasters. Hand in hand, they level the playing field. We can't say we trust God and balk at obeying Him. Some things are clear obedience calls in Scripture, such as purity and profession of faith. Others are per-sonal, and you alone know how closely aligned you are to God's heart and call.

Therefore, I bless you, _____, to begin with the smallest acts of obedience that begin to cut convenience out of your life. Inconvenience is often God's intentional way of breaking your de-pendence on your own resources.

Someone needs encouragement, and God's asking you to respond? I bless you to do so, even when it's not convenient.

Something He's asked you to give? I bless you to give with a cheer-ful heart, even if it's clearly not convenient.

Someone He's asked you to forgive? I bless you to forgive as Jesus forgave you, even though it is definitely not convenient.

I bless you, _____, to do so—without complaining, without negotiating.

I bless you to do so with a thankful, cheerful heart.

I bless you to do so with the expectation that it will cost you some-thing.

And I bless you to do so with the understanding that God will back you with His strength, His compassion, His love and His Spirit.

Really.

I bless you, _____, in the name of God, Three-in-One, whose thoughts are not yours, whose ways are higher, so much so that when you surrender your convenience, He will beckon you into a deep dependence that is incredibly greater, more exhilarating and far more courageous than a superficial life of convenience.

Notes (anything I need to do/think differently/consider who needs to hear this, etc.):

Testimonial/feedback: "I have personally been able to both receive and to bless others with the blessings. I have felt encouraged and refreshed by them; and, when they are read to me, I am often deeply encouraged by listening. I love that they are rooted and grounded in God's Word. Because they are steeped in Scripture, I often choose to go deeper into studying the passages in the blessing and get blessed again!"

Blessing 65: Splendor

Your life, _____, sparkles with the splendor of your Savior. It's a glorious life, one which cannot be dimmed by disappointment or caught off guard by a moment of weakness, because in all things, you, _____, are more than a conqueror through Him who loves you (Romans 8:37).

Selah, _____. Pause and calmly think on that. The love of God broke through the claims of darkness and swept you into the kingdom of God for His goodness led you to repentance (Romans 2:4). God loves you in surpassing ways that do and will overtake you on occasion with sweetness, inspiration, tender emotion, over-whelming joy and pulsating radiance.

I bless you, _____, to ponder each and every love-trans-forming encounter in your heart, much like Mary, poring over them with wonder. And I bless you—out of the overflow of your heart—to speak volumes of life into the hearts of others. For you have been called to do exactly that.

_____, you display Jesus.

You brood over and meditate on His word, for it is your delight (Psalm 1:2), and in it you find the Living Word who speaks with clarity and intention—and you draw constantly from Him your sustenance and joy for the day and the night ahead.

You speak words of refreshment and hope to weary souls who long for not just a listening ear, but an attentive heart that desires to speak as John wrote of Jesus: *"It is the Spirit who gives life; the flesh profits nothing. The words that I speak to you are spirit, and they are life"* (John 6:63).

I bless you, _____, to articulate in tune with the Spirit's passion and His leading, so that your integration of wisdom and words continually resonate kingdom decrees. I bless you to speak with the courage and the cadence of your Master. And I bless you with God's astuteness in regards to timing, depth, and deliberation of the words you speak. You have His ear, and He has your tongue —a critical combination for spiritual advancement.

You, _____, reverberate the splendor of the Lord. And such reflection is gloriously spoken of in Scripture.

I bless you in the name of the Father, the Son and the Spirit who inspired the prophet Malachi to speak these life-giving words which speak of you: *"Then those who feared the Lord talked often one to another; and the Lord listened and heard it, and a book of remembrance was written before Him of those who reverenced and worshipfully feared the Lord and who thought on His name. 'And they shall be Mine,' says the Lord of hosts, 'in that day when I publicly recognize and openly declare them to be My jewels (My special possession, My peculiar treasure). And I will spare them, as a man spares his own son who serves him'"* (Malachi 3:16-17, Amplified version).

_____, you are a resplendent jewel, and you are blessed indeed.

Notes (anything I need to do/think differently/consider who needs to hear this, etc.):

Testimonial/feedback: "I was read this blessing this past year on my birthday. The Lord used it in powerful, tender ways to minister to my heart. I didn't even realize how much I was in need of encouragement until this blessing was read over me. I was going through a difficult time physically; but, as a result of my spirit being touched in such precious ways by my heavenly Father, I was strengthened! Praise the Lord!"

BLESSING 66: THE KINDNESS CALL

_____, kindness is your calling as a child of God. Look at your heavenly Father and note how His kindness is called out in Scripture:

Joel 2:13 states: *"So rend your heart, and not your garments; Return to the Lord your God, For He is gracious and merciful, slow to anger, and of great kindness; and He relents from doing harm."*

Nehemiah 9:17b reiterates this same understanding: *"But You are God, ready to pardon, gracious and merciful, slow to anger, abundant in kindness, and did not forsake them."*

God asks us to be like Him in this: *"But love your enemies, do good, and lend, hoping for nothing in return; and your reward will be great, and you will be sons of the Most High. For He is kind to the unthankful and evil"* (Luke 6:35).

You, _____, are kind because God has shown you great kindness.

I bless you to be stretched to the uttermost in this calling for then you will break through others' hardness of heart. Have you ever noticed that harshness never garners you the response you desired? It's not a call to speak only easy words, but it is a call to speak them with the heart of the Father. Difficult words can have great effect but only when tenderized by love.

And yet, God summons us to go beyond the speaking and do some hard things that reveal His kind heart. Ephesians 4:32 instructs us to *"be kind to one another, tenderhearted, forgiving one another, even as God in Christ forgave you."*

You, _____, excel in forgiving, because you comprehend the forgiveness of God. You love the unlovable and those who have harmed you, because you long to exhibit Jesus to them. You do good, because that is God's nature, and He is alive and in you. You give, because He is the Giver and gives generously; and so you also reflect His generosity with cheerfulness and gratefulness.

You are His. You have been bought with a price and are not your own.

Your new nature, your new way of living and breathing and doing life is Spirit-empowered to shout kindness to the world, starting with those closest to home and then expanding to those who wouldn't even care to call you. I bless you with the compassion and tenderness of the Shepherd as you live out your calling with glory-infused excitement, for you will stand out as one untouched by deception and animosity. You will radiate kindness.

I bless you, _____, in the name of the only God—Father, Son and Spirit—Who is kind and good, merciful and compassionate, ever-loving and ever-giving and who blesses you with His incomparable nature so that you will speak and live and love as He does and unearth His glory to a world in desperate need.

Notes (anything I need to do/think differently/consider who needs to hear this, etc.):

BLESSING 67: REFRESHING

Are you in need of refreshing? Sometimes life is a bit stale or maybe even downright depressing or disheartening. Biblical heroes weren't exempt from such times. David wavered; Jonah felt the heat and Paul persevered during intense emotional, physical and spiritual struggles. They needed the Lord's touch and His presence daily, and so do you. So I bless you, _____, to draw from the limitless well of God's love, power and peace that alone can bring restoration and refreshment to your heart and soul.

I bless you, _____, to take great comfort in the fact that you cannot escape the presence of God. *"Where can I go from Your Spirit? Or where can I flee from Your presence?"* called out David in Psalm 139:7. Even in Old Testament times, the truth was told that God was present.

And now—in New Covenant theology—we believers have the living God *within* us. So when down days threaten or they intrude unwelcomingly, we need to drink deeply from God inside, the Spirit who pours out rivers of living water.

So drink, dearly beloved child of God! Drink deeply of His love. Thoroughly drink of His strength. Partake with wonder His joy. Soak deeply in His grace and compassion and allow them to pour into your very being.

You were made to be refreshed—and to wake renewed, to live revived and to rejoice at your very core.

Because it doesn't happen automatically, don't automatically assume that it's not for you. Proverbs 11:25b reveals one secret for those who yearn for deep, well-watering refreshment. *"He who waters will also be watered himself."* Or, as the NIV renders the verse: *"Whoever refreshes others will be refreshed."*

Isn't it just like God to turn your refreshment into a party? YOU reach out to others, and you will reap the marvel of more than one life transformed by God's touch. So I bless you, _____, to reach out in faith to bless others with refreshment.

A kind, wise word…

A gentle touch…

A compassionate note at just the right moment…

An anonymous gift…

An offense overlooked…

Fervent prayer in the secret place…

A heart-spoken encouragement...

The possibilities beckon you to participate.

God will direct you as you take the lead on the path toward refreshing others, watering them with His grace and His compassion.

And you, _____, will be blessed with a deep, thankful, gracious drink that will breathe life into your very being. Suddenly, you and the one or two or three that you have refreshed and watered will be party to the outrageous grace of the God who never leaves you and always has your best at heart.

So I bless you, _____, in the name of Jesus, who calls you to a well-watered, unquenchable joyous journey of refreshment that draws other sojourners into the celebration.

And as you do so, your legacy will include the blessing that the Apostle Paul and Timothy wrote to Philemon and the church that met in his house: *"I always thank my God, _____, as I remember you in my prayers, because I hear about your love for all His holy people and your faith in the Lord Jesus. Your love has given me great joy and encouragement, because you, _____, have refreshed the hearts of the Lord's people"* (Philemon 1:4-5;7 NIV).

Notes (anything I need to do/think differently/consider who needs to hear this, etc.):

BLESSING 68: CALLED

You, _____, have been called by God to do more, think more and pray more than you could ever be able to do on your own. The word *"called"* implies both reception and action. You have been open to God's call on your life. You listened and received His call with open ears, heart and hands.

Then you hearkened to His call to minister with the specifically unique expression of the gifts He has granted you. Today you stand as a testimony of a faithful listener and doer; and, according to James 1:25, you will be blessed in what you do.

You, _____, have been expressly chosen to be an exceptional instrument of God's love and heart. Your position of influence is intentional in God's sight. Your long hours, enthusiasm, service and dedication stand out as a reflection of God's goodness.

Colossians 3:16-17 is descriptive of what you do, so let these verses ring in your heart as a reminder of what God has called you to: *"Let the word of Christ dwell in you richly in all wisdom, teaching and admonishing one another in psalms and hymns and spiritual songs, singing with grace in your hearts to the Lord. And whatever you do in word or deed, do all in the name of the Lord Jesus, giving thanks to God the Father through Him."* You are devoted to fulfill this calling, and God is pleased with your faithful response.

Along with the Apostle Paul in Philippians 3:12-14, I encourage you to press on, that you may lay hold of that for which Christ Jesus has also laid hold of for you. Do not count yourself to have grasped it yet; but this one thing do: forget those things which are behind and reach forward to those things which are ahead—and press toward the goal for the prize of the upward call of God in Christ Jesus!

You are strategically placed to spiritually advance the kingdom. This call on your life is no small matter. It is backed by the force and the power of the Spirit, for you have been called out of darkness into light.

It will propel you to be a luminous light and to become increasingly radiant as you learn and grow and minister to those who need the transforming power of the Spirit to break strongholds and gain territory for the kingdom of Jesus—the kingdom that has no end!

So I bless you, _____, to grow in God's grace. I bless you to reveal His nature—God's greatness and goodness—to a world in desperate need of a God vision, a Jesus revolution and a Holy Spirit takeover.

I bless you to *"study and be eager and do your utmost to present yourself to God approved (tested by trial), a workman who has no cause to be ashamed"* (2 Timothy 2:15a, Amplified Bible).

I bless you, _____, in the name and the power of Jesus, who is called *"Wonderful, Counselor, Mighty God, Everlasting Father, Prince of Peace. Of the increase of His government and peace there will be no end"* (Isaiah 9:6b-7a). You are called to walk, run, learn, grow, flourish, advance, triumph and rejoice in the blessing of His calling!

Notes (anything I need to do/think differently/consider who needs to hear this, etc.):

"My husband and I were able to take this blessing to Uganda and speak it over the administrators, teachers and children who work at and attend the nonprofit Christian school we were blessed to help start. Graduation ceremonies are incredibly important in Uganda—and this ceremony celebrated many children who could not afford to go to school (even public schools cost money to attend, so many never get the opportunity). As my husband read the blessing, I was so encouraged to see the faces of the children and adults alike light up with hope for what God has in store for them and their future."

BLESSING 69: FRUIT FINDER

What if the Holy Spirit sent you on a treasure hunt to discover Him at work? You, _____, would be on the lookout for fruit (of the Spirit, that is). What joy to uncover instances of exhibited love in families (instead of family feuds)! What a blessing to see the Spirit freely deposit kindness into an account at your work, allowing an overflow of abundance to impact your co-workers, customers and supervisors!

I bless you, _____, to be a fruit finder.

It's easy to be a fault finder. But how marvelous to be a fruit finder —and oh, so biblical. Hebrews 3:13 puts it this way: *"But encourage one another day after day, as long as it is still called 'Today,' so that none of you will be hardened by the deceitfulness of sin"* (NASB).

And from Hebrews 10:24-25: *"Let us consider how to stimulate one another to love and good deeds, not forsaking our own assembling together, as is the habit of some, but encouraging one another; and all the more as you see the day drawing near"* (NASB). So I urge you daily to notice the beautiful work of the Spirit in your own life and the lives of others—and to point it out with pleasure.

For example, patience is often sorely lacking in today's society— which is why it is one of the most sought-after and prayed-for personal requests, but the Holy Spirit isn't deficient in longsuffering.

So I encourage you, _____, to allow the Holy Spirit access to your emotions so that you will *"wait upon the Lord"* in every situation that concerns you and receive the blessing of Isaiah 40:31: *"But those who wait on the Lord shall renew their strength; they shall mount up with wings like eagles. They shall run and not be weary; they shall walk and not faint."*

Likewise, I urge you to applaud the Spirit's work in other believers' lives as they exhibit patience in the place God has them. Be sure to affirm them and mention the Isaiah 40:31 promise.

Peace frequently accompanies patience in those who are led by the Spirit. Peace is noteworthy in its propensity for stillness. *"Be still, and know that I am God; I will be exalted among the nations, I will be exalted in the earth!"* (Psalm 46:10) is the perspective of those who give ear to the Spirit's call to surrender self and allow God His magnificent place over every situation that distresses them.

Therefore, I exhort you, _____, to heed that still, small voice of God that encourages you to lay your cares and burdens before Him. I pray that you will frequently observe it in others. Then you can join them in prayer and thanksgiving that precedes the Spirit's overflow of peace in guarding their hearts and minds in Christ Jesus (Philippians 4:7).

And what about faithfulness? Be on the *"look out"* for this treasured fruit, and call attention to it— whether it's revealed in small or great ways. Faithfulness in marriage, in friendship, in giving, in serving, in standing when the temptation is strong to give in or give up— all reflect the Father.

I encourage you to speak words of Spirit affirmation into the hearts of others who are faithful. Your words may be a catalyst for resplendent renewal.

As you, _____, choose to encourage, exhort and bless those whose lives display the fruit of the Spirit—whether in marginal or monumental amounts—you'll discover that you will be speaking and walking in tandem with Jesus and His heart for people.

You will find yourself more apt to go with the flow of the Spirit over your own emotions. You will emulate Jesus as you exhort and stir others to do the same.

So I bless you, _____, in the name of the Father, who gave you the gift of the Spirit; in the name of Jesus, His Son, who rose triumphant and returned to heaven so that you would be endowed with the Spirit's presence and power; and in the name of the Spirit, who indwells you and generously gives you His fruit so that your life will blossom, flourish and—in turn— bear much fruit.

Notes (anything I need to do/think differently/consider who needs to hear this, etc.):

BLESSING 70: YOUR DEFENDER

Isn't it a blessing that you do not have to passively wait until you figure out the right fix-it formula or push the correct "rescue me" button? God is your refuge and strength, your ever-present help in time of trouble (Psalm 46:1). You do not have to defend yourself.

I bless you, _____, to see the Lord fight on your behalf during trials and testing. See your God safeguard you from false accusations and from condemnation. Trust that God will be glorified by keeping His promise to use for good and redeem what the enemy will try to spin into destructive lies against you.

Your defeated enemy is as tireless as the ocean tide, and he rushes in with the same old falsehoods that bolster insecurity, self-doubt, fear and shame. I bless you to push back with a holy peace and security in your identity and promised protection in Christ. Jesus came to destroy the devil's work (1 John 3:8). I bless you to not get in His way.

Therefore, I encourage you, _____, to resist the enemy, and he will flee from you (James 4:7). King Jesus disarmed your enemies and made a public spectacle of them, triumphing over them by the cross (Colossians 2:15).

God has promised—actually, He takes it up a notch—He *rejoices* to do you good (Jeremiah 32:40-41). Do you ever imagine being as the one who is "greatly loved" in Daniel? Three times in Daniel, the angel Gabriel came and told him he was "greatly loved." Or how about being considered "the one whom Jesus loved" spoken of in the gospel of John? I bless you to picture yourself as being greatly loved.

For He does love you…deeply.

So revel in His preserving power. Stand firm in the shelter of the bulwark. Allow the howling winds to war against your Defender's sanctuary. I bless you, _____, in the name of the Most High God, who is at the ready to take on the one who threatens to destroy you—for your God has the last word.

Notes (anything I need to do/think differently/consider who needs to hear this, etc.):

16082547R00117

Made in the USA
San Bernardino, CA
18 October 2014